MW01273650

Julia McCoy

~~CONTENT~~ ~~BURNOUT:~~ CREATE CONTENT

How Entrepreneurs Can Position Their Voice & Brand
in the World Without Overload, Frustration, or Burnout

ISBN paperback: 9798403550697

Visit Julia McCoy's website: contenthacker.com

Learn more about The Content Transformation© System: contenthacker.com/transformation

Contents

Foreword

By Joe Pulizzi

In March of 2007 I left my fancy executive publishing job to start a business. What was the business, you ask?

It was amazing, actually. I'll describe it as "the eHarmony for content marketing." I know, right? Pretty cool. Basically, I was going to match up companies that needed content services with agencies and writers that provided those services.

But with little money and a lot of programming ahead, I believed the best course was to build an online audience first. So, on April 26th, 2007, I started my blog called the "Content Revolution." Three times a week, every week, I wrote an article about how marketers could be successful with content marketing.

At first it was awfully quiet. As the months went by, I literally had dozens of subscribers to my blog. My best customer was my mom, who read each blog post religiously (even though she didn't have a clue what I was writing about).

Luckily, I knew building an audience with content takes time. I persisted.

In June of 2008 I finally launched the matching product. I bought search keywords. I advertised on social media. I even exhibited at trade shows.

By September of 2009 the writing was on the wall. We were bleeding cash, and although the idea for the business was sound, the market just wasn't there yet.

I made the decision to close up shop. Even worse, I decided to stop my entrepreneurial journey and go get a "real" job.

As I was dusting off my resume and LinkedIn profile, I looked at my blog subscriber list. That's right, I never stopped writing.

I now had a couple thousand subscribers that seemed to value the content I was producing.

I thought, "what if I focused on really building that audience, and then developing a business model around that audience?"

After a discussion with my wife, I decided to give it one more try. I developed a business model, which is almost exactly like the process you'll read about in this book.

In early 2010, then with almost 10,000 subscribers, I renamed the company Content Marketing Institute (CMI). Being near burn-out levels as a content creator, I started to outsource many tasks I didn't like or wasn't great at. I brought on a managing editor. I hired a search specialist. I recruited a designer and a web strate-gist. And thankfully, I found someone to oversee the day-to-day activities so I could focus on creating remarkable information for my audience.

By 2016, CMI became the leading online destination for content marketing, developed the #1 print publication (*Chief Content Officer* magazine) and claimed the world's largest in-person event for the industry, Content Marketing World, at 4,000 at-tendees per year. And we had well over 200,000 avid subscribers to our content.

That same year, my wife and I sold the business for over $20 million dollars.

Now I'll be honest, this model is not easy. It takes time and patience. You need focus and consistency.

Everyone is a publisher today. Everyone creates content. There is clutter everywhere. But very few actually develop a process and a strategy that builds a successful content-first business model.

You'll find that process in the pages of this book.

I've known Julia for almost a decade now. She was there while I grew my business and then sold it for an amazing exit. I had the same pleasure to then see her grow her incredible brand and choose a million-dollar plus exit.

You have in your hands, on your kindle, the plan I didn't have when I began my journey.

Oh, what I would have paid to understand and know the process in advance.

You don't have to make three years of mistakes like I did.

After my successful exit, I took some time with the family and wrote a mystery novel...but I couldn't stay away. I'm doing it all over again at my new startup, The Tilt, helping content creators become content entrepreneurs. And guess what? I'm using the strategy from this book to do it.

Building a business with online content is the fastest growing business on the planet. That's right, you are definitely not alone. But, you are one of the few that already know the secrets to success.

Be Epic!
Joe Pulizzi
@JoePulizzi

Founder, The Tilt and Content Marketing Institute

Introduction.
FROM CONTENT BURNOUT TO A MILLION-DOLLAR EXIT & LIVING A FULFILLED LIFE

Since I started my writing agency, Express Writers, back in 2011 with just $75... all the way towards our million-dollar exit ten years later in 2021—there has always been that one turning point I can look back to and say, *that was it.*

One action that changed everything.

One step that took me from scraping the bottom of the barrel to the heights of success I barely dreamed of.

How did I go from the mess of those early years—overworked, scrounging for leads, wheels spinning endlessly—to the smooth-sailing ship I built and exited?
Content.

More particularly, a **content strategy** with **planning, processes, and delegation** working together as vital pieces.

(Because content alone gets you nowhere. Print that out and hang it on your desk, write it on a Post-It, tattoo it on your fore-head: Friends, marketers, entrepreneurs... CONTENT ALONE IS NOT A SOLUTION.)

If you're reading this, you're probably at least semi-familiar with my story at Express Writers.

Before my exit, the content marketing I strategized and led pulled in 99% of our leads. We did it all without investing in a single paid ad. The big mindblower: in less than seven years, my agency reached $1,000,000 in annual sales.

I've transitioned out, but when I ran it, we lived by selling what we did and doing what we sold. It was beautiful, and the best sales machine I think one could ever create. I built our blog, before selling blogging services to clients; and then continued to stay committed to posting long-form, educational content to our blog, week after week. Our story of $4M (it's now more than that) in sales through an inbound content marketing approach has been featured in Forbes.[1]

In my journey, I've had the honor of being a featured speaker at Content Marketing World,[2] taught content workshops for eight-figure brands, and have written guest columns for Entrepreneur, Content Marketing Institute, MarketingProfs, Semrush, Search Engine Journal, and more. I've written six books[3] (you're reading the 6th). I've built and taught three courses[4] on content marketing, strategy, and writing. I've run not one, but THREE blogs: the Write Blog,[5] the Content Strategy & Marketing Course Blog,[6] and currently, the Content Hacker Blog.[7] Recently, I condensed everything I do and built a new training program that will be 100% of my focus going forward. Inside my transformative incubator-like system, with a self-led pathway and hands-on coaching, I now help entrepreneurs and the next generation of business leaders grow their digital brands and presence through strategy, skills, and systems into a lasting presence and revenue. Learn more about The Content Transformation© System at contenthacker.com/transformation.

Today, my content marketing (and by extension, my business) hums along at a steady pace, gaining ground consistently, *because* I found a way to overcome my burnout. The truth is, it wasn't always this good. You'll read about my near-failure moments in the pages ahead. It was when I invested in and built what mattered: smart processes, a good team, and the right tools, that content began to *work for me*. Not the other way around.

We publish one blog per week, EVERY week, rain, snow, shine, or any other scenario withstanding. It was our rule at Express Writers, and it's my rule now at Content Hacker every single week.

I never question what to delegate, what not to delegate, or who to delegate to. I spend only ONE day per week setting up my content plan for the month.

Here's the best part... If I step away to spend an afternoon with my daughter or relax with my family, my content *keeps working* in the background.

At Express Writers, we reached over 100,000 visitors in one month with this strategy; and I'm repeating this success story with the same approach at Content Hacker, a newer brand/domain I acquired in 2019 and am building from the ground up. Before my exit, Content Hacker was my side hustle; and even then, we sold $400,000+ in courses and training. Today, I've removed all the piecemeal and created my ultimate Content Transformation© System, a brand growth incubator training program. I'm repeating the same approach I used at Express Writers at Content Hacker, but in a harder niche, harder business model, and tougher marketing lane. *And it's working.* I'm able to step away and play with my kiddo, husband, and dogs, while my amazing team at Content Hacker takes calls, converts prospects, and guides them on orientation in our new coaching program. (All of that happened in one morning just this week. I was completely hands-off and simply encouraged my team in Slack!)

The thing is, what I've achieved *isn't* the lone diamond in the coal mine. I hope I've proven to you by simply sharing my story that it's possible for anyone. This is not a unicorn situation. It's transferable. It's repeatable. And it can work for YOU. Creating content strategically. Getting results. Without burning out, stressing out, or wasting resources.

It's. All. About. Strategy.

That's what I'm here to teach you in *Content Burnout.*

Are you currently sitting in a shell of a boat that's slowly leaking, with no rudder, no map, and no way to steer?

Are you barely staying afloat instead of making headway through the rough waters of building your business?

More importantly... Are you ready to rethink content creation?

Because I'm ready to show you everything I know.

Let's do this.

Chapter 1.
HOW TO RETHINK THE CONTENT CREATION PROCESS IN TERMS OF SUCCESS

"It's hard work. I'm not going to lie. Anyone who tells you that it's really easy to build a content business is not telling you the truth. You have to accept the fact that this is going to be grueling, difficult, time consuming, and laborious work. But if you're willing to roll up your sleeves and get dirty, and are willing to constantly analyze what you're doing and scrap what doesn't work and continue what does work, and keep at it, you can be very, very successful."

– Michael Stelzner, *founder of Social Media Examiner*

Picture this...
It's a Monday.
I want you to CHOOSE your morning.
Pick road a or b...

(Yes. This isn't a drill. Take out your pen, and physically check-mark next to A or B.)

☐ **A. *The Non-Burned Out, Smart Creator:*** You're drinking your first cup of coffee. The sun is shining... the birds are singing. Your kids are home for the summer, and you have plans to take off and check out a new dinosaur exhibit an hour down the road later in the day. You're relaxed, at ease, *excited* to see how your thriving business is doing today. You've done the work to grown it 100% through ad-free, holistic marketing you love and identify with, that is compounding on itself over time; and you've done the work of setting up a team, systems, and processes that also work.

First, you check in on Slack. Your amazing team is up and at it. They were clocking in before you woke up—a couple of them live in opposite time zones to you. They're producing already, re-capping an early meeting they had with a new prospect. The prospect is ready to put down $5k on your program. The lead converts and buys shortly after you check Slack. Looks like your team is scheduled to have five more calls with ideal client fits today, producing an estimated $15k in new sales over the next seven days.

You look at your content calendar. All is well. The next two months of content are planned, because of that two-hour planning sesh you completed last Friday with enthusiasm. Your writers are on their assignments, and tomorrow's blog is currently under the red pen of your blog editor and will go live tomorrow at 10 a.m. Boom. Time to head to the dinosaur exhibit with your kiddos.

☐ **B. *The Burned-Out, Overly-Exerted, Inefficient but Hardworking Creator:*** You're on your third cup of coffee. You have five calls you're trying to rally yourself for, coming up soon, the first one looming ahead in thirty minutes. After that, you *still* have your own content calendar to try and resuscitate—you're badly behind on your blog—along with tasks to partially deliver for your clients, because the two people on your creative team haven't been pulling their weight lately. You're trying to breathe, but the caffeine you've inhaled is making you jumpy—or is it the stress of the day ahead?

The obvious answer most people will choose is A. Why wouldn't you want a productive morning with a business running like clockwork? Option B makes my muscles tighten up just think-ing about it, but it's the reality for most entrepreneurs and biz owners (and it was for me for many years, too).

Look at the data: Only 30% of businesses will survive to reach their 10th year of operation.[8] That means a whopping **70% fail** be-fore they gain any longevity. And **64% of content entrepreneurs** say **burnout** is a real problem.[23] And it's no wonder, considering the tension and stress they endure every single day they man-age to keep their ship afloat. They're running on fumes—and burning out fast before they can reach stability and security in their enterprise.

Another factor working against the creator who wants to grow through content is simply summed up in this one point: GREAT

CONTENT ISN'T EASY. Approximately 94% of all web pages get zero backlinks.[10] 90% get no traffic *at all*.[11] *Yikes*. But when you're up against that wall where you want to create content that earns ROI, you want to do it right, but you don't have the support, resources, or time to make it happen... Enter burnout. Enter option B. You never chose it, but somehow, you end up there anyway.

Sadly enough... This is all too common. Most people *want* option A... but choose option B unconsciously.

Because it's not a matter of waking up one morning and deciding to get it together with your business and work life. You can't snap your fingers and make option A happen instantaneously. Instead, option A is the result of the tiny, seemingly inconsequential decisions and choices you make day after day, week after week.

But that's the good news. You DO, in fact, have a choice. And I'm here to tell you Option A is *totally, completely, and truly* a very possible reality *YOU* can achieve.

Know you have the power to choose your alternate future as a creator. You do not have to be the burned-out, typical, inefficient yet well-meaning, hard-working content creator. You do not have to be part of the 70% who fail before gaining a foothold in their target market. You can be the smart creator, checking on your efficient business and *crushing* it without burnout, before breakfast.

Okay? It's possible. Stop telling yourself that first scenario is a dream. It's not.

It's. A. Strategy. Away.

This is what *Content Burnout* is all about.

And once upon a time, I was you. The burned-out, hamster-wheel creator-slash-entrepreneur.

Before: Steering the Ship with No Map, Wheel, or Rudder (No Content Strategy, No Delegation, No Nothing)

When I first started my writing agency, Express Writers, there was so much I was doing wrong.

Before, I was attempting to steer the ship of business-building with no map, no ship's wheel, and no rudder. If you can imagine a shell of a boat, floating adrift in stormy seas, with me frantically trying to move the boat by paddling with my hands, you get a good idea of what it was like.

My efforts were fruitless. I barely made the ship move where I wanted it to go. More often than not, I was too busy bailing water out of the bottom to focus on forward movement.

I was "doing" content marketing, but it looked like this:

I tried to publish blogs every day, but the pressure of that schedule made me lax about quality.

I often pushed out content just to get it "out there."

My content wasn't getting results.

I tried to do cold outreach for leads to make up the difference, but those efforts were utterly wasted and turned up zilch.

My email list was sad and lonely. My emails were unwanted. They often cried alone in dark corners.

I had my hands in a billion different pots but wasn't seeing any ROI from all that effort.

I was working 12-hour days just to "do it all."

The leads I *did* get were crappy, to put it lightly.

In a nutshell, I was DONE.

Overworked. Stressed to the max.

Fed up. *Tired.* And honestly? It's no wonder. Here are the results I was getting, two years into the game:

I had published 215 blogs on my site... but only had 141 keywords ranking at the top of Google.

My business brought in an average monthly gross income of $29,000.

Site traffic peaked at 500 visitors/day.

Growth was sluggish at best. It wasn't enough. We weren't cruising through the choppy waters of business-building or making headway. We were barely staying afloat.

But a few things happened next that led to my content breakthrough.

After: What Happens When You Wise Up

What happened?

My writing agency reached a breaking point. And that breaking point ended up changing my life.

Weirdly enough, it started with an epic failure. In fact, a failure *so* grandiose and epic, that I will never forget the day, time, place, and meal I was eating when it all came crashing down (vivid trauma memories, anyone?).

In May of 2016, on a Mother's Day weekend, I made a shocking discovery. I found out the two managers I'd trusted for years were embezzling from my company. That was just the beginning of how deep this horrible iceberg ran. Not only were they stealing money, but they'd been intentionally trying to bring us down and dismantle us by inserting typos in my writers' content, while building a clone of my business on the side all along hoping to funnel all our clients there. My content wasn't working... and now, I find that all the trust I'd placed in the top members of my team was *misplaced*. Talk about a harsh wakeup call. It was one of the most brutal moments—ever—in my entrepreneurial journey. I'll never forget that Friday night when the whole burning fire just erupted and it felt like I was sitting in flames, as my husband and I worked quickly to delete their accounts in our business systems. Things hadn't been going well, to begin with—as we already mentioned, my content wasn't bringing in a ton of leads—but finally having to face the fact that the two people I'd trusted and paid to run my company at a high level had been stealing thousands during payroll for eight months, sabotaging our writer's assignments, and then emailing our clients from their new writing agency drawing on the relationship they'd built under *my* company name to try to steal these clients out from under us—well, go ahead and try to picture a worse scenario in any business. Try.

I had to stop, regroup, and rethink *everything*.

Including the way I was running and marketing Express Writers back then.

It was either pivot or die, literally—so, we pivoted.

First order of business: Build a better team. We did that. It was brutal and painful, and it continued to take me years to learn which person fit in which role. (For instance, before I exited, my best salesperson was a former editor. She had a 90% close rate on her calls. This blew my mind at the time. Today, it makes complete sense to me to put an editor in a sales role, because the product knowledge she has is amazing—she used to edit content and see our writers' talents firsthand. We figured that one out through trial-and-error.)

Second order of business: build, plan, and execute a content strategy. A real-life editorial calendar, with birds-eye publishing dates mapped out wisely weeks ahead of time (yes, I had slacked on building one for years). Content topics mapped out to our audience's real pain points. Personas that really matched our real-life target audience. A clear SEO (search engine optimization) strategy that brought us leads that followed blog CTA (call-to-action) breadcrumbs into our ecommerce Content Shop, interacted with our knowledgeable, kind, but not overly salesy inbound sales team, and then placed a content order with us. (Sometimes those initial orders could be $10,000 at a time.) In other words, our content worked. Our team worked. Our business worked. And we made revenue. It was a dream come true.

That initial momentum turned into rocket fuel for us.

In just the first few months after I implemented a content strategy (managing and delegating a plan instead of flying by the seat of my pants, doing it all myself), with a better team in place...

We earned over $71,000.

We almost doubled our keyword rankings in Google from the previous year (3,900 to 6,000).

We saw the highest shares on our blogs to date.

And the wins didn't stop.

We continued to see record income months. *Month after month.*

We started ranking top five for hot keywords in our industry. (Like "copywriting services." Whaaa?)

Our web traffic jumped to thousands of visitors/day.

Since 2011, I haven't missed my publishing goal of 1 blog/week, come rain, sleet, or shine. Without a content strategy, without managing it all versus doing it all, I never would have been able to maintain that content load.

In 2017, I set about to teach practical content marketing for business profits. My journey began when a client called me up one day to ask: "Julia, can you *please* start teaching what you know?" He asked me to come to his office and teach his staff. I declined, not feeling ready–I had zero curriculum prepared. But that call launched me into market research, writing my first nonfiction industry guides, and the early start of what I have today:[24] my coaching and consulting business at Content Hacker, where I've taught thousands of marketers how to get great at content. After enrolling over 1,000 people in 13+ courses and programs I built, and listening to their pain points along the way, I condensed all of my concepts and created a new training system with five phases that is nothing short of **lifechanging**. It's THE single training program for brand builders that want to implement a slow, steady, *sure* approach with a clear content marketing strategy, and team delegation/growth techniques put into place that simply *work*.

In this system, I give creative entrepreneurs EVERYTHING they need to build and grow a digital business that will last for years to come. It's called The Content Transformation© System, and you can learn more about it at **contenthacker.com/transformation**. We only work with creative entrepreneurs, founders, and aspiring/established business owners that are **ready to hit their next level in business freedom and do what it really takes to get there**. If that's you, I'd encourage you to consider applying today.

Today: A Lean, Mean, Content Marketing Machine

If you're reading this, you're probably at least semi-familiar with my story.

Our content marketing pulls in 99% of our leads. We do it all without investing in a single paid ad. The big mindblower: My agency has brought in $1,000,000, yearly. Today, Express Writers is a thriving business I grew from scratch—and recently handed off successfully to new owners in a million-dollar sale. My agency has been known for selling what we do and doing what we sell. We were grown *through* content—and we sell great content. (Our story of inbound growth has even been featured in Forbes three times.[1])

Today, I'm doing the same thing in a tougher market, tougher vertical, and niche. I'm building Content Hacker to 1M visitors/year and 1M in revenue with repeatable processes, systems, and a SINGLE powerful coaching program. Selling a coaching program is much more in-depth than selling agency services, I've found. Yet, by repeating the same content marketing approach, strategic business techniques, and growth/team systems, we're on track to reach my goal inside the next 24 months. I'm doing all this in 2022, while pregnant with our second child due in March.

Getting here took a lot of hard work. It took a seismic mindset shift. But I got here. **I made it.** *I'm doing it again.* And you can, too.

Brace Yourself for a Mindset Shift

Let's pause right here. Before I go on, you need to know the most important piece of my story is not the success I eventually achieved. Sure, it's nice to have, and everybody eyes those glorified success goalposts—mounds of money, less stress, and faster growth—with want and envy, but none of it is the point. For me, the eventual wins never would have happened without one crucial moment: when I pivoted and shifted my mindset about how to create content and grow through methodical planning, strategy, and delegation.

That pivot saved my business life. I would not be where am I without it. Embedded in that shift were some crucial ingredients, too:

ACCEPTING the way I was going previously was leading directly to failure.

DREAMING of success, and setting BHAGs in place (Big Hairy Audacious Goals, a concept coined by Jim Collins[9] in his book, *Built to Last*—more on this later).

WISING UP about what I needed to do to reach that castle in the clouds—defining goals, finding my brand and content differentiation factors (CDF), and building plans for growing my business.

PARTNERING UP with the right creators, managers, and other experts who could help me execute.

INVESTING back into my business as I went forward.

How to Rethink the Content Creation Process and Pivot

ACCEPT your old methods don't work.

DREAM of success, and dream big (Big Hairy Audacious Goals).

WISE UP about how to reach those goals.

PARTNER UP with the right content creators, managers, and other experts.

INVEST back into your biz as you move forward.

Content Hacker™ / Julia McCoy

Let's examine each of these steps in more detail: ACCEPT, DREAM, WISE UP, PARTNER UP, and INVEST.

ACCEPT Your Old Methods Don't Work

Old habits die hard. This cliché aphorism is cliché for a reason. It's true. The habitual way you've run your business and done your marketing in the past isn't working. It hasn't worked. It won't work in the future. That said, it's hard to let go of those habits, let alone change them. In the same way, it's hard for your great uncle who's smoked cigarettes for 20 years to quit smoking, or for that friend of yours to lose 50 pounds after spending their 20s eating mostly junk food.

Hard, but not impossible. That's why it's so important to fully acknowledge bad habits and bad methods. To change them, you must admit them in the first place, accept they don't work, and move forward to build better ones. If your great uncle or your friend had just ignored their bad habits, they never could have summoned the mental capacity needed to change them. You can't change what you don't think is a problem.

Don't just take it from me. In his bestselling book, *Atomic Habits*, James Clear[17] tells us exactly how habits are formed, good and bad. As he says, "The seed of every habit is a single, tiny decision." The small, seemingly insignificant decisions you make day after day, week after week, month after month, become your habits, and your habits determine where you end up. If you backtrack from where you are today, can you see the tiny decisions you made that helped you get here? Can you see how each turn in the path, each choice, built on the one before it? Can you see how they might have led to a business or endeavor that's sinking versus sailing?

Compounding bad habits leading to near failure for a business is a common occurrence, unfortunately. The story of Leigh Paints, a U.K. business[18] that manufactures and sells industrial paint, is a prime example. It's also a fantastic case study in accepting where bad habits can land you, pivoting, and changing for the better.

Leigh Paints didn't just sell paint—they made and sold protective coatings responsible for shielding the steel frames of high-rise buildings from melting in fires, and preventing corrosion on industrial structures like oil platforms, military ships, airport terminals, bridges, and wind farm equipment.[19] The company was over 100 years old, founded in 1860, but by the late 1990s, it was circling the drain. Why?

It refused to change. Particularly, Leighs' management methods and habits were entrenched in bureaucracy and inflexibility, totally unsuitable for 21st-century business. The marketplace was changing, seemingly by the day with the advent of the internet, but Leigh Paints was not.

However, by 2008, the company had made a turnaround. Employee satisfaction increased by an average of 19 points across areas like internal communication, teamwork, and management style. Staff turnover decreased by 10%. Absenteeism decreased from 8% to 1.8%. The company was working better, too. They saw 288 service complaints in 2000, but by 2008, they had 95 total—a 67% drop.

What happened?

A change in habits from the top down, the very thing they had been fighting all along.

Leaders at Leighs finally took action in the face of a dying company. The Board of Directors replaced the three managers at the top who had been splitting duties and appointed one person as the Managing Director and CEO, a man named Dick Frost, who they tasked with turning everything around. It was a tall order for one person. In his search for guidance and inspiration, Frost stumbled upon Steven R. Covey's *The 7 Habits of Highly Effective People*. It lit a fire under him.

With this one book serving as a guide, Frost enacted a revolution of change. He bought copies for his entire executive team, who were buoyed by the ideas in the book and realized they could make change happen across the entire organization, transforming the company culture so it would not just survive, but thrive in the 21st-century marketplace. Any managers who still resisted changing their attitudes or behaviors were replaced. Because that's exactly where they started: with the managers. With themselves and the way they were guiding (or not guiding) their employees. They started with habits.

These were the habits and methods that, over 140 years, had led to "managers reporting to managers who reported to managers," to a "hierarchical, industrial-age organizational matrix," according to the case study[18] written for FranklinCovey's Center for Advanced Research in 2009 (FranklinCovey is the publisher of *7 Habits*). In this environment, employees were treated as cogs in a machine. They were expected to do their work the same way every day, no deviation allowed. If they had suggestions on improving the company, their ideas got lost in a maze of bureaucracy. Most showed up to earn a paycheck and expended just enough effort to do their appointed tasks. For a lower-rung worker, it must have been a bleak, demoralizing place to work.

But the managers and top brass committed to change. They established BHAG (Big Hairy Audacious Goals—I talk about how amazing these are in the next section) at every level of the company and aligned them so an overarching sense of purpose reigned throughout the organization for the first time in decades. They established goal-tracking so everyone, top to bottom, could monitor progress. Company leaders took corporate culture training courses and started welcoming employee feedback and suggestions. What's more, they even started actively *helping* good ideas reach the top, where they could be implemented. Lastly, but perhaps most importantly, employees started getting invested in the company's goals because they had a hand in them. They were given autonomy to improve their workplace, and they took it further than anyone expected: Workers reconfigured and repainted work areas, and their suggestions to add windows to key spots were implemented.

It wasn't a snap-your-fingers change. It took a while—a handful of years at least—but the company's culture improved. Along with it, so did profits. So did customer service. So did employee satisfaction, as well as the products they sold.

This is a fairly drastic example of how acceptance of change can change your business, but it's an important one. It doesn't matter if you sell industrial paint or marketing services—if your old business habits aren't working, nothing is going to save you unless you acknowledge your trajectory and shift gears in response. After that, you *must* implement change, one painful step at a time.

It's mind-altering once you realize how off-track you might be from where you *want* to be. The good news is, you can change course today. Right now. This very second. You simply have to understand where you went wrong and make the commitment to alter your course in the right direction. Since habits are formed in the tiny moments and decisions that happen whether you notice them or not, you can start forming good business habits, content creation habits, marketing habits, and growth habits in the same way.

Let's return to *Atomic Habits* for inspiration:

"The seed of every habit is a single, tiny decision. But as that decision is repeated, a habit sprouts and grows stronger. Roots entrench themselves and branches grow. The task of breaking a bad habit is like uprooting a powerful oak within us. And the task of building a good habit is like cultivating a delicate flower one day at a time."

– James Clear

DREAM of Success, and Dream Big

HOW BIG do you want to go?

HOW BIG do you want to set your goals?

Don't be afraid of dreaming loud and big. Go crazy. Dare to dream in technicolor versus simply black and white. Set a clear, huge goal, one that has apparent and actionable steps you can start taking right now to reach the finish line. As I mentioned, I live by the principle of the BHAG[9] (Big Hairy Audacious Goal): a goal that's BIG, clear, compelling, and urgent. This kind of goal requires you to build towards it day by day. Thinking about it makes you excited and anxious (in a good way) to get going, and raring to see that future materialize on your horizon.

The BHAG has growth embedded in its DNA. Jim Collins, the author of *Built to Last* and the inventor of the concept, provides a few great examples of BHAGs: NASA's mission to reach the moon in the 1960s. Boeing's vision to build a large commercial jet aircraft in the 1950s.

In this excerpt from *Built to Last*, Collins describes[12] the BHAG like so:

"Like the moon mission, a true BHAG is clear and compelling and serves as a unifying focal point of effort– often creating immense team spirit. It has a clear finish line, so the organization can know when it has achieved the goal; people like to shoot for finish lines.

A BHAG engages people– it reaches out and grabs them in the gut. It is tangible, energizing, highly focused. People 'get it' right away; it takes little or no explanation."

In other words, this is the smart way to dream. Because you *can* get what you want—you *can* create content without burn-out and grow your business exponentially—as long as you stay shrewd, practical, and strategic about the pathway you must take to achieve that dream.

Speaking of goal pathways. BHAGs are smart, but they're also SMART. If you've never heard of this acronym, here's what it stands for:

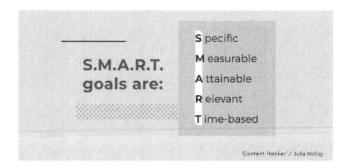

Specific: The goal is clear, obvious, and tied to a person, place, or thing. When you hear it, you get it. You know what the crowning desire is at the heart of the goal. (If the desire is muddled, the goal is not specific enough.)

Measurable: The goal should use a goal *post* that's trackable. That means you can use metrics to determine whether you've met it, made it, or reached the finish line.

Attainable: With the right tools and resources (ones you can feasibly acquire if you don't have them), you can reach the goal.

Relevant: The goal aligns with your business and overarching objectives. It makes sense.

Time-based: You can realistically meet the goal within a specific time frame.

Hold your BHAG up against these criteria. Does it meet all of them? If not, tweak the goal until it's SMART.

A name directly tied to BHAG-type dreaming in content marketing is Michael Stelzner. He's the founder of a little site called Social Media Examiner, which happens to attract millions of visitors per year. The thing is, when Michael started in 2009, he knew absolutely nothing about social media marketing. He was a writer who made his name crafting whitepapers for big brands. He was miles away from any deep understanding of Facebook or Twitter. He only knew there was huge potential brewing within the social media industry.

What was it? Nobody was sharing deep, specific, "how-to" details about social media for free on blogs or websites. Michael saw a giant hole waiting to be filled, and he dreamed of creating a site that would become THE resource for social media marketers and small businesses.

One small snag. Back in 2009, only five years after Facebook launched as a social network for Harvard students and three years after it expanded to the general public, two entire years before Instagram existed, there was *no such thing* as the social media marketer we know today. Social media platforms were still finding their footing, and brands were just starting to realize the possibilities for using social to reach their audiences. To become a major name in this environment, not only would Michael and his team need to break new ground into a new industry, but they also needed to attract a niche that was in the beginning stages of sprouting.

It was the epitome of a BHAG. Here's how Michael described it in an interview[16] with Experian:

"It was about creating a movement. It was about embracing others. It was not about us."

They hit their goal with a bang. Two weeks after SocialMediaExaminer.com launched, Technorati rated the blog as one of the Top 100 Small Business Blogs. One year later, the site had earned over 40,000 email subscribers and $1 million in revenue.[13] Today, the site enjoys 2 million+ visitors per month, about 450,000 email subscribers, and remains the largest digital publication on social media marketing in the world.[14]

It's a case study in crushing your big goals and fulfilling your big dreams. It's a star example of creative, strategic, incredible content marketing.

"We've built something really, really fascinating, all on the back of a premise that if you provide valuable insight, people will want more, and they will be willing to exchange that insight for an email address. With those email addresses, you can build a multi-million-dollar business."

– **Michael Stelzner**[14]

WISE UP About Reaching Your Goals

As we all know, dreaming of success isn't enough to make it.

The most important bit of Michael Stelzner's story isn't how Social Media Examiner won. Instead, the most vital part to pay attention to is *how.* How did they utterly smash it in such a short amount of time?

We know the dream of turning Social Media Examiner into the ultimate social media marketing resource was a BHAG, which helped immensely. On top of that, Michael and his team were **wise** concerning how they went about reaching it.

👉 **Note**: The definition of *wise*[15] includes a few points, according to Oxford Languages: "1) Having or showing experience, knowledge, and good judgment. 2) Responding sensibly or shrewdly to a particular situation." Wisdom isn't just about being **wise—wisdom is all about how you *respond* to a situation**. It's about action: physically using your smarts as you build toward your goals! That's KEY.

Social Media Examiner's wisdom looked like this:

They defined specific, practical KPIs (key performance indicators) for their overarching goal of creating a hot, ultimate resource—like reaching 40k email subscribers within one year.

They defined a unique, emerging niche to target (social media marketers, who were novel in 2009).

They differentiated from other content creators by offering amazing, free, helpful, "how-to" content (according to Michael Stelzner, nobody was giving away this kind of content for free back then).

They wanted to create higher-level content than the standard in place in 2009. Instead of 200-word blog posts, they wanted to double, even triple, that length to create incredible depth in their content.

At every point, they defined concrete, clear KPIs that ultimately would help them achieve their larger goal. They eked out unique factors that would differentiate Social Media Examiner from similar online publications. Particularly, they defined their content differentiation factor (CDF for short), which was how they set themselves apart from competitors with the types of content they published and delivered.

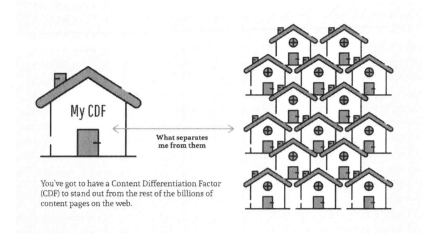

You've got to have a Content Differentiation Factor (CDF) to stand out from the rest of the billions of content pages on the web.

Your **differentiation factor** is a key tenant to know and define to stand out and build long-term authority in your industry (or help your client achieve, in theirs). It's one of the first parts to nail within a strong content strategy.

Building a differentiation factor that will set your brand apart for years to come is one of several key business skills I integrate into all the brands I launch. I teach this skill with hands-on mentoring in The Content Transformation© System. **Learn more and apply today: contenthacker.com/transformation**

Ultimately, Social Media Examiner offered a unique solution to a growing problem in the industry. Nobody was offering free, in-depth advice, guidance, tips, and tricks on successful social media marketing. Social Media Examiner and Michael Stelzner stepped in, and the rest is history.

The takeaway? Don't just set goals. Set *smart*, Big Hairy Audacious Goals that inspire action. Then, wisely start working to reach them. Take practical steps. Find unique angles no one else has thought of. Set deadlines to hit and metrics to reach. Define those KPIs. Wise up about reaching your goals, and they'll become infinitely more doable.

PARTNER UP with the Right People

Do you currently have your hands in every pot? Are you chopping the vegetables, simmering the broth, browning the meat, seasoning the pot, *and* serving the soup, all while keeping the kitchen clean and planning next week's menu?

Just as no chef works alone in any commercial, high-production kitchen, nor should you do the work of two, or three, or five people by yourself. You can *oversee* a ton of different jobs, but you shouldn't be doing them all. You have one brain, one pair of hands, and two eyes. Growing a business (versus just maintaining a business—and yes, there's a giant difference between the two) is no joke. It will take everything out of you: time, money, patience, your sanity, weekends, your savings, and maybe even your last nerve. You were not made to do everything alone. And if you try, you'll be left solo in that rowboat without an oar, paddling with your hands and drifting in circles.

At the beginning of my journey, 2012-ish, I was *Express Writer,* before I was truly *Express Writers.* It took a random call with a business coach that year to make me realize I had to stop doing everything myself and learn how to delegate and hire. Once I began delegating, I stopped spinning my wheels doing everything, and went from owning a rowboat to creating the underbelly of what could now be called a cruise ship (40,000+ completed projects, 100+ contracted team members on board).

This is one element that trips up many well-meaning business owners. You have an idea, a dream, and no one loves that burgeoning, blooming concept more than you. You need it all done right—so you have to do it yourself. Or, you don't think you can spare the investment to hire help. So, you float on alone and exhaust yourself.

Here's the solution. As soon as you decide to signal S.O.S., as hard as that is; as soon as you invest in partnering up with the right people, it starts paying off immediately. It's like somebody swims over to your boat and climbs in... But hold on—they're not just a random stranger. They knew you were stranded and they brought a paddle!

At that moment, you'd probably cry with relief. You're so tired, on the brink of collapse, and your dream isn't growing. The shores of success never appeared within your viewfinder before. But now, with help, you can start moving toward that horizon in the distance. You don't have to waste all your energy on paddling anymore. *Thank God!* That freeing feeling is exactly what partnering up with the right providers does for you and your business. Solo-it no more, my friend. Your one-woman, one-man days are over.

 Experts Chime in: Joe Pulizzi, founder of Content Marketing Institute & The Tilt – *thetilt.com*

> *Joe Pulizzi* is a marketing great, known the world over for his skills. He's authored six books on content marketing, including the best-sellers *Content, Inc., Killing Marketing*, and *Epic Content Marketing*. He's the mind behind one of the foremost content marketing events, Content Marketing World. Here are his thoughts on the mistake of "doing it all":
>
> *Too many content creators feel they need to do everything for their business... all the content, the planning, the marketing, the business side. It's natural to want to take everything on... and is also a huge mistake.*
>
> *Take a sheet. On one side write down the tasks you love to do or are really good at. On the other side, write down the things you do not like or are not good at. Then, over the next six months, find contractors and freelancers to do all those things so you can focus on the things you are great at. Another tip: what's your exit strategy? A content entrepreneur should have an idea of the proper exit when they start their business (seriously). Of course, this can change over time, but without having an idea of where you are taking the business, burnout can happen quickly.*

👉 You can't just hire anybody; I know better than anyone that it's a feat to find the right somebodies. All the nitty-gritty details on partnering strategically, hiring the right people, and delegating well are tucked inside **Chapter 2: How to Successfully Delegate & Partner with the Right Resources.**

INVEST Back into Your Business

The final step in your mindset shift should be embracing the idea of investing in yourself and your business at every stage of the game.

It doesn't matter whether you're starting with barely any overhead or are sitting at the helm of a million-dollar company. Investing back in as you make headway is key.

Let's think back to our little rowboat. Once you have some paddles and another person to help you row toward your goals, take whatever extra income you make and invest it back in. Patch that small hole in the floor. Spring for some hats and sunscreen for you and your partner. Add cushy seats and a life preserver. You get the picture.

When you're bootstrapped to the nth degree, how do you invest in your business? However you can.

A fact I'm not shy about sharing is that I started Express Writers with $75. Picture it—that's just three twenties, a ten, and a five-dollar bill. It was all I had left in my savings, at the time. I was 19. I didn't even have enough money to buy my own brand-name domain at the beginning. Can you believe that? I let expresswriters.com hang out there for almost eight months, because I didn't have $600 at the time to buy it. But I didn't let that discourage me.

Starting with very little is not just *okay*, it's *doable*. The only way to go is up. As I earned my first clients and started making money, I invested that right back into my business. It was one of the best investments I ever made. Little by little, I was able to invest more and get more out of it. Just as building your personal savings is a smart move for your future, so is putting at least some of what you earn back into your operation. Whether you invest in hiring another team member, buying a domain, enlisting professional website design or expert copywriting for your main sales page, or new equipment or software to improve your processes, it's all worthwhile.

Now? I drop $4,000 on my coach in one invoice.

$2,000+ on my writers every month.

$1,000+ on my designer every month. (Some months, that number looks like $2,800.)

$5,000 per year – sometimes more – in domain names and hosting.

Thousands on programs and software to make my team better.

I don't blink when it comes to dropping dollars for the sake of my business. I know it's worth it and will make my business better, or my team better, or my processes better, which will ultimately increase my earnings overall.

Sara Blakely, billionaire, entrepreneur, and inventor of the women's shapewear phenomenon, Spanx, started her $1 billion business with a mere $5,000 in savings.[20] She had a vision for a product that was totally novel and needed, but missing from the hosiery market: a lightweight undergarment any woman could wear under clothes, totally undetectable but comfortable, which would smooth and shape the body.

But in the beginning, *nobody* got Sara's vision. And Sara hustled. She cold-called hosiery mills to ask for help developing her product idea, but they were all run by men who, it turned out, really didn't understand what women wanted or needed out of hosiery, which is partly why pantyhose hadn't changed since its invention in 1959 by—you guessed it—a man.[21] Finally, after too many failed phone calls, after Sara physically drove from Atlanta to North Carolina's hosiery mills to convince someone, *anyone*, to help her make her product, one mill owner reconsidered. He had told his daughters about the product, and they persuaded him it was, in fact, a brilliant idea.

What followed was a year of prototyping, writing her own patent with help from a book she bought at Barnes & Noble, since hiring a patent lawyer would eat all her savings, and designing the product packaging on a graphic design friend's computer. She didn't know how to write the legal claims portion of her patent, so she convinced a lawyer to do it for a discounted $700. She couldn't afford marketing, so she knew she had to make her package "scream" at people from the store shelves (she made it bright red to stand out in a sea of beige, the standard for hosiery packaging at the time). She attended endless meetings with buyers and sales associates at department stores, pitching them Spanx. She sent product samples to important people, including Oprah's stylist, Andre Walker...

...Which is how Spanx ended up on one of Oprah's famed "Favorite Things" episodes. In November of 2000, Spanx was Oprah's favorite product of the year.[22] From there, Spanx was unstoppable.

Sara Blakely's success absolutely had to do with the combination of her $5K investment and her can-do attitude. She saved money wherever she could and used the rest strategically and smartly until Spanx started making money—$4 million in its first year.[22] Once she could afford marketing, she dove right in, investing in traveling to do in-store demos and appearances on local news stations. She landed a coveted deal with QVC after they read about her in Forbes, and she even generated buzz when she appeared on a reality show for entrepreneurs with Richard Branson, where she finished as the runner-up.

Today, Spanx earns $400 million in annual revenue and is a household name. But, remember: A great product will only get you so far. Smart decisions will take you further, as Sara Blakely's journey illustrates.

Whether you have $75 or $5,000 to invest back into your business, it's important to not just think about putting your money where it will count, but to *do* it in the first place.

It's easy to promise, but hard to carry out in principle. Saving and investing don't come naturally to a lot of us. If we have extra dollars, we want to spend them on fun, or on physical things that will make our lives better, or on splurges that give us a rush of happiness in the moment. But I'm imploring you *not* to spend your extra revenue on throwaway items or one-time luxuries. Put those dollars and cents back where they'll count instead of indulging in a fancy dinner at a restaurant. Buy new software for your biz instead of buying new clothes. Invest in hiring an additional team member instead of taking that mini vacation. Hire a content writer to improve your content marketing versus buying a round of drinks for your friends.

The sacrifices you make now will allow you to do everything you want later. One day, you won't have to make a choice between smart investments and creature comforts. One day, you'll have both—but only if you're smart NOW.

"You've got to visualize where you're headed and be very clear about it. Take a Polaroid picture of where you're going to be in a few years." – Sara Blakely, Spanx founder & entrepreneur

Chapter 1 Wrap-Up

- You have the power to choose your future as an entrepreneur.

- First, you have to make a giant leap—a mindset shift about what success actually looks like and how to get there.

  » ACCEPT your old methods aren't working. You can't change what you don't think is a problem.

  » DREAM of success differently—the smart way. Dare to dream of Big Hairy Audacious Goals.

  » WISE UP about how you'll reach those goals. Get strategic. Define KPIs. Look at your CDF (content differentiation factor): what is it? How will you demonstrate it?

  » PARTNER UP, because you shouldn't do it all alone. Hire people to help you execute. Let go of total control, and get a team running who will stand behind you.

» **INVEST** back into your business as you go along. In the beginning, this won't be much, but as you gain success, you'll be able to build on it faster if you invest in your enterprise.

Next up: Let's delve deep into how to partner up and delegate strategically in **Chapter 2** to blast apart burnout for good.

Introduction & Chapter 1 References

1. Joe Escobedo. "How To Attract $4 Million In Client Revenue Through Content Marketing." (2018, Jan. 7). *Forbes*. https://www.forbes.com/sites/joeescobedo/2018/01/07/how-to-attract-4-million-in-client-revenue-through-content-marketing/

   Joe Escobedo. "Convincing Executives To Buy Into Content Marketing Is All About Demonstrating Value." (2018, Feb. 20). *Forbes*. https://www.forbes.com/sites/joeescobedo/2018/02/20/how-to-convince-executives-to-buy-into-content-marketing-by-demonstrating-value

   Melissa Houston. "From Growing Up In A Cult To Building A 7-Figure Business." (2021, May 19). *Forbes*. https://www.forbes.com/sites/melissahouston/2021/05/19/from-growing-up-in-a-cult-to-building-a-7-figure-business/

2. Julia McCoy. "Building a Tangible Website Content Strategy: A Beginner's Guide." (2020, May 14). *Content Marketing World*. https://www.contentmarketingworld.com/julia-mccoy-building-a-tangible-website-content-strategy-a-beginners-guide/

3. https://contenthacker.com/books/

4. https://contenthacker.com/academy/

5. https://expresswriters.com/write-blog/

6. https://contenthacker.com/create-a-content-marketing-strategy/

7. https://contenthacker.com/blog/

8. U.S. Bureau of Labor Statistics. "Survival of Private Sector Establishments by Opening Year." (2020, March). https://www.bls.gov/bdm/us_age_naics_00_table7.txt

9. Jim Collins. "BHAG." https://www.jimcollins.com/concepts/bhag.html

10. Brian Dean. "We Analyzed 912 Million Blog Posts: Here's What We Learned About Content Marketing." (2019, Feb. 19). *Backlinko*. https://backlinko.com/content-study

11. Tim Soulo. "90.63% of Content Gets No Traffic From Google. And How to Be in the Other 9.37% [New Research for 2020]." (2020, Jan. 31). *Ahrefs*. https://ahrefs.com/blog/search-traffic-study/

12. Jim Collins. "BHAG – Big Hairy Audacious Goal: *Built to Last* Excerpt (Coauthored with Jerry I. Porras)." https://www.jim-collins.com/article_topics/articles/BHAG.html

13. Jim Armstrong. "Interview with Michael Stelzner, Founder of SocialMediaExaminer.com." (2011, July 7). *BrandYourself*. https://brandyourself.com/blog/social-media/inter-view-with-michael-stelzner-founder-of-socialmediaexamin-er-com/

14. Joe Pulizzi. "Michael Stelzner from Social Media Examiner (281)." (2021, June 3). *Content Inc with Joe Pulizzi* [Podcast episode]. https://www.contentinc.io/michael-stelzner-from-so-cial-media-examiner-281/

15. https://www.google.com/search?q=wise+definition

16. Experian. "Small Business Guide to Social Media: Interview with Michael Stelzner." https://www.experian.com/small-business/michael-stelzner

17. James Clear. *Atomic Habits: An Easy & Proven Way to Build Good Habits and Break Bad Ones.* (New York: Avery, 2018), 22. https://jamesclear.com/atomic-habits

18. Dean W. Collingwood & Sangita Skilling. "Changing Colours at Leighs Paints." (2009, Feb.). *FranklinCovey Center for Advanced Research.* https://resources.franklincovey.com/success-stories-the-7-habits/changing-colours-at-leighs-paints

19. Sherwin Williams acquired Leighs Paints in 2013, but retained their employees. It was a lucrative deal for both historic companies. https://www.prweb.com/releases/2011/7/prweb8622669.htm

20. Inc. "How Spanx Got Started." (2012, Jan. 20). [Video transcript.] https://www.inc.com/sara-blakely/how-sara-blakley-started-spanx.html

21. Joseph Caputo. "50 Years of Pantyhose." (2009, July 7). *Smithsonian Magazine.* https://www.smithsonianmag.com/arts-culture/50-years-of-pantyhose-33062523/

22. Claire O'Connor. "How Sara Blakely of Spanx Turned $5,000 into $1 billion." (2012, Mar. 14). *Forbes.* https://www.forbes.com/global/2012/0326/billionaires-12-feature-united-states-spanx-sara-blakely-american-booty.html

23. The Tilt. "2021 Content Entrepreneur Benchmark Research." (2021, Apr.-May). https://www.thetilt.com/research

24. Julia McCoy. *Practical Content Strategy & Marketing.* (2017). https://amzn.to/3oYqPYp

25. https://contenthacker.com/content-transformation/

Chapter 2.
HOW TO SUCCESSFULLY DELEGATE CONTENT & BUILD THE RIGHT RESOURCES

"If you want to do a few small things right, do them yourself. If you want to do great things and make a big impact, learn to delegate."

— *John C. Maxwell,* *leadership expert, author, & speaker*

You've done it. You're here. You've made the mindset shift necessary to start moving forward and finally growing your enterprise, in a way that *won't* burn you out. Because you finally know it's possible.

You're in the right spot to turn things around for the better. To supercharge your growth efforts, including your content and your business.

The mental shift you made to get here wasn't the most difficult bit, though.

No, no—it's yet to come.

One of the hardest parts, for a lot of people, is this one. The next step we're about to dive into headfirst.

But this part is also one of the most vital.

Delegation. (*dun dun *dun**)

Why are people so scared of delegating? Yes, *scared*. A survey by the Institute for Corporate Productivity of 332 companies found that about half of them were worried about their employees' ability to delegate. However, only 28% offered delegation training.[1]

Another study covered in Harvard Business Review[2] discovered that knowledge workers spend about 41% of their time on "discretionary activities"—ones that offer little-to-no personal satisfaction, tasks that could be accomplished more competently and efficiently by other workers. This particular study was pretty wide-ranging—it looked at 45 different knowledge workers across 39 companies and eight industries. Unfortunately, the way the vast majority spent their time at work was disheartening.

The researchers found that even those workers deemed super-performing wasted tons of time on "tedious, non-value-added activities." In other words, they frittered away precious hours on desk work and low-value meetings instead of engaging in work that lit their fire, that they excelled at and loved to do.

Sound familiar?

It's early morning on a Monday. The birds are chirping outside in a welcoming rhythm, the coffee is brewing, and you're about to dive straight into your workday.

A couple of tasks are already throwing themselves at you, vying for attention and begging to get done. One is especially important. You need to write the weekly post for your company blog. It needs to be done by tomorrow morning so it can go live at the scheduled time, 10 a.m.

Why isn't it done, yet? Because you can't bring yourself to hand it off to a writer. *I need to be able to do this*, you think. There are too many nuances to writing your business's blogs and you don't have time to relay them to someone else. Only you intimately know how you want the blogs done.

The only problem? Time ins not on your side. You know your topic and industry like the back of your hand, but *writing* the dang thing is a different animal altogether. You are so distracted with immediate tasks in the business that you put off writing them many times. You have that Instagram live your business friend invited you to do later today, and you have a coaching call with one of your clients just after that IG Live. Exasperated, you finally write one in a rush, dashing off bland introductions and so-so copy you hope is adequate. You side-eye the blog as it goes live, and wonder if it's readable.

The ones you write are good enough, right? At least you included some keywords in the last few you posted.

It's all very wrong, no better than a shot in the dark, and we haven't even covered the worst part. You're so close to your blog post writing, you can't even see that your blogs could, in fact, be *miles better*. In fact, they could be huge vehicles for leads and sales—written faster and better, with less headaches, less teeth-gnashing, and more skill. They could be optimized better, written with better flow and readability. They could be more engaging. They could pull in more desired customers, convincing them of your expertise, products, or services.

If only you'd hand the creation tasks off to someone else. If only you'd invest in content.

Sound familiar? If the studies tell us anything, it's that you're not alone. You're not the only business showrunner clinging to tasks you should be handing off, even when you know you're not doing a great job. Hey, even I was guilty of this at the beginning of my journey.

Of course, the big questions—*why* are we so resistant to delegating? *Why* do we insist on wasting our own time?—are hard to answer. The Harvard Business Review study authors, Julian Birkinshaw and Jordan Cohen, reason it this way:[2]

"Because ridding oneself of work is easier said than done. We instinctively cling to tasks that make us feel busy and thus important."

Sometimes, we get too close to our work, whether the task is big or small. When the stakes are high all-around—when you're just starting and trying to turn a profit, have been struggling to stay out of the red, or have to work like mad for every client or every sale—each task feels like life or death, whether you're pitching to a major prospect or writing one measly blog post.

Unfortunately, treating every single task as equally important is a *terrible* way to run a business.

Your time is valuable. The way you spend it matters. That's why delegation is so essential.

How Delegation (A.K.A. Getting Help) Revolutionizes Your Content Creation Process

Delegation is necessary for every square inch of your business, but *especially* for the content creation part of content marketing. That's because truly good, worthwhile, ROI-worthy content needs a special kind of care, attention, and qualified skill that you may not have.

Let's address the elephant in the room. That content you're constantly rushing to get out? The times when you shrugged your shoulders, muttered "good enough", and hit "publish" just to get something live on your social feed or your blog?

It's not good enough.

It won't turn into traction for your brand or company.

"Done is better than nothing," you say to yourself.

The cold truth is, doing nothing _would_ be more worthwhile to your happiness and joy than rushing content creation and publishing sub-par work. Let's unpack why.

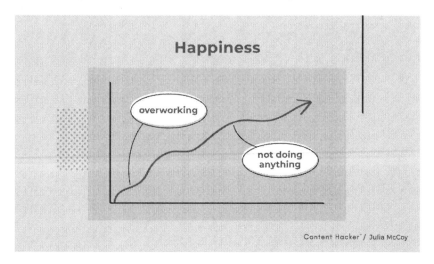

Content Hacker™ / Julia McCoy

Rushed content is _never_ good content. Rushed content is sloppy. Rushed content always has errors. It isn't polished. It isn't researched well enough. It's not thorough and is often unsatisfying to read for the user with questions about your topic.

Rushed content is choppy and reads like someone brain-dumped their ideas on a page and called it "good enough" (which, let's face it, is _exactly_ what happens when you're rushing).

Rushed content will never, ever outperform content that was developed over time. Slap-dash content will never do better than well-edited, researched, honed content with good flow, fully formed ideas, strong links, and attention to detail. Are you uncovering the theme? To be worthwhile, to earn ROI, to bring in leads and traffic from Google, content needs a few things: space to develop, expertise to assemble, and time to refine.

Let's repeat that: If you want truly high-quality content, it requires **expertise to assemble, space to develop, time to improve and refine**. And a burned-out marketer/business owner frantically trying to do it all—publish blog posts, social media updates, videos, emails, etc. *every week* will NOT produce anything of quality with only one, or two, or *none* of those things, to devote to their content roster.

Let's break down these three requirements further.

Expertise

High-quality content DEMANDS a skilled, knowledgeable writer. A writer not only needs knowledge on the topic they're writing about but also real skill in their craft of SEO writing. This is a double shot of expertise that not many people have. (Sure, you've been working in finance for five years. Sure, you can write any old content. But do you have the additional skill to write so Google ranks your content and readers give it the time of day? If not, you NEED to learn that skill to get results. *By the way, I teach everything I know about crafting SEO content at seowritingcourse.com.*)

Space

Once your writer has the two-fold skill set necessary to write quality, results-getting content, the next element they need is space: space to let ideas develop, space to go down research rabbit holes to bolster their writing, space to turn brain dumps into fully formed thoughts. This space is essential because it's when ideas coalesce into something concrete. During this time, your writer is probably locked into various states of *flow*, or the super-fruitful, creative time when their work bursts into being, a "trance-like altered state of total absorption and effortless concentration," according to Hungarian psychologist Mihaly Csikszentmihalyi.[9] Without space, achieving a state of flow is impossible. And, without flow, content greatness rarely happens.

Time

Last of all, we come to the time factor. For content writing, too much time is better than too little. While some people can certainly create quality content in a crunch, imagine how much better their work could have been if they'd just had a few more minutes or hours! Once the ideas are formed and on the page, writers need time to comb through them, refine them, and hone them into something better. Many writers will tell you without hesitation that their least favorite part of the job is editing, but, crucially, editing is what turns mediocre work into *incredible*, impactful work. I'd even argue that great writing happens during the editing stage—*not* during the writing stage, when the goal is just to get words and ideas out of our heads and recorded so we can play with them, then hone them into something coherent, and, hopefully, exceptional.

Space, expertise, and time. Your writer needs all three to do their best work. Of course, their best work = work that gets results. Content that ranks. Content that pulls in readers and turns them into loyal customers. Because content absolutely should do some incredible heavy lifting for your brand as a whole.

As you can see, creating content is a lot like baking a fancy loaf of artisan bread. It's hard to get right. It's needy. It's finicky. You can't produce it in one shot, one day, or one hour. In fact, creativity expert and writer Jeff Goins[3] says our brains simply can't handle the mind circus that happens when we try to fast-track what should be a long process.

Content needs space. It needs time. It needs a creator devoted to their craft of writing. And it needs expertise. If you're doing it all yourself, even though you might have the expertise, you may not have enough of the other factors to make it work.

What should you do instead?

You need a **PROCESS** that spits out amazing content day in, day out. You need to start Monday mornings knowing exactly what's going out on your blog on Tuesday, and preferably, stay about three weeks ahead of schedule. But, you also don't have to sit down and plan out an entire year of content (in fact, that could bleed you dry in terms of appearing "relevant" – fresh is always better).

You need to be able to step away from your process without worrying whether it will collapse while your back is turned. You need to be at the helm, giving it some well-timed nudges and bigger pushes now and then, but the ball should keep rolling even when you're not around.

Just *where* do you get your writers?

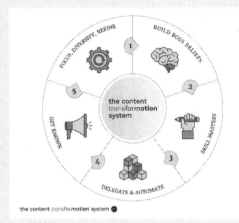

the content transformation© system

the content transformation system

I teach the strategies, systems, and skills involved in first knowing how to put together a delegation-ready content marketing strategy, then secondly, being able to find/hire/manage your writer or writing resource inside The Content Transformation© System.

Hiring and managing your own writers *successfully* is a multi-step pathway. *Before* you hire a writer, you should know what to do first in order to plan and then delegate your entire content calendar to your writer. Otherwise, it's confusion and mayhem galore, and the content produced is typically unusable (without it being the writer's fault). Inside my system, you will gain clarity on all of the steps that precede writer delegation, then learn how to find, hire and manage your perfect-fit writer.

Watch our free training explaining The Content Transformation© System and learn more about how to set up a winning content strategy, delegate your marketing, and create long-term brand success at: contenthacker.com/transformation

The way to achieve that (utter content freedom, you might say)?

Partnering up. Thinking in terms of **managing**, instead of doing.

It's a big mindset change, but you need to start thinking this way now. Otherwise, as an entrepreneur focused on growing your business and scaling through content, you'll burn out fast.

What's the secret to managing your content instead of doing it all and burning out before you gain any momentum?

Delegation. It's all about **DELEGATING** your ideas to a trusted content partner!

This means:

You must take off the "writer" hat and set it aside. You have to give up control of the nitty-gritty "creation" part of content creation.

Giving up some of your creative control can be difficult, yes. But – it will free you up to do bigger, better things with your time. Integral, incredible, business-building things. Stuff you'd NEVER be able to do while stuck creating content in a giant hamster wheel.

Ask yourself: What will you GAIN in return for outsourcing and delegating the work?

First, remember what investing in expert content nets you in terms of growth. HubSpot studies have found that marketers who prioritize content marketing efforts are 13x more likely to see serious ROI from their marketing.[10] On top of that, SEO content drives 1,000% more traffic than organic social media marketing, most likely because 68% of all online experiences begin with a search engine.[11] I.e., when somebody opens up their browser—and, by the way, 31% of American adults are online *constantly*[4]—the first site they head to is Google (or YouTube, which is just a Google-owned video search engine).

Online content is where it's all happening. Hordes of consumers are on the internet, and they need content. Not to mention, committing to content is proven, with proven rewards. And, there's only one action you need to take to start reaping your share: **Do content right.**

More than eight-in-ten U.S. adults go online at least daily

% of U.S. adults who say they go online ...

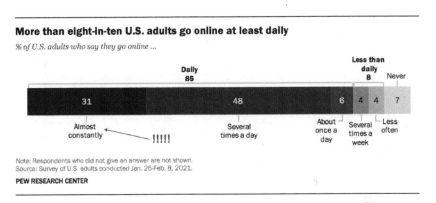

Note: Respondents who did not give an answer are not shown.
Source: Survey of U.S. adults conducted Jan. 25-Feb. 8, 2021.

PEW RESEARCH CENTER

How do you do content right? With delegating, you don't have to worry. You'll get an expert—and if you're not a writer, you'll get someone better than you, who can produce better work than you'd ever achieve alone—and they'll use their knowledge to get it done and do it right.

Then, remember what delegating also does for your time. *It frees you up to do bigger things.*

Win, win, win. You'll get real ROI from your content, because an expert will be handling it, and your time will be freed up so you can do bigger things.

If you want to scale, you MUST get help. (I'll get into more about **who** should be helping you later in this chapter.)

Think of it this way.

You can work for your content...

OR your content can work for you.

Your choice. What'll it be?

Why You Must Invest to Make Delegation Work

Delegation isn't as simple as turning to someone else and saying, "Here. I need you to do this." Nor can you wake up one day and say, "I'm going to start delegating!" and then instantly have it figured out.

Invest in the Process

Delegation is a process. It's not one-and-done (which you'll soon see is a theme running throughout this entire book; in fact, my brand The Content Hacker™ is built on the principle there are no hacks to business growth—*hacker* simply represents getting to those long-term strategies in the SHORTEST time possible).[17] There are steps to climb, doors to open and shut. You must implement delegation in stages, because delegation requires a lot of moving parts, each with its own necessary pieces. First, you need the right people to delegate to. (This is HUGE. More on this aspect in the next section.) Then, you need to ensure you share the same goals and understand each other's expectations. Your team member—employee, or contractor, or freelancer, or partner—must know what you want to get done AND how to do it well, with minimal intervention on your part. This will take time and training while they develop those skills. None of this happens overnight, and none of it happens without some effort, planning, management, and investment.

Invest with Serious Dollars

Yes, delegation is an investment. If you want to compete in your industry, be prepared to invest in your entire delegation process. Get ready to hire the right people, train them well, pay them fairly, and empower them to handle what you delegate. In short, you must put in dollars and hours for superior partners, superior work, and superior content.

Thankfully, you only need to invest a finite amount of time. Once you get the ball rolling, it can and should keep rolling without you. That means, once you train and empower a partner, once you've delegated the right way to the right person, it's enough. The next time you need the same or a similar task completed, the employee, team member, contractor, freelancer, etc., should have the skill to handle it again with little oversight. (Wouldn't that be *incredible*?)

Unfortunately, even though many are embracing it, many more pass over the opportunity to invest in delegation. "I'm a creator," they say. "I can do it better." *Can you?* I'm a writer, and I still hire out my writing tasks every week to *other* writers who work with me. I do this because **delegation is an opportunity**. The half-assed tasks you're rushing now, with little time or expertise to do them right? Those could be completed with finesse and downright *pizazz* by someone else, faster and with fewer headaches. For marketing tasks like content creation, you could be missing a big chance to make your marketing magnificent, and by extension to grow your business exponentially, just by investing in other people and handing off a bunch of tasks.

Because, truly, the delegation investment is an investment in the future of your business—it's just disguised because the pay-off isn't immediate.

Do you have to spend $10k to self-publish a book, like I do every time I produce my books? (Writing, research, and editing: $5,000–$8,000. Formatting for Amazon: $500. Audible narration by an expert: $2,500. Book cover and inside illustrations: $1,500.)

No...

But...

You SHOULD if you want to compete and make a difference! You SHOULD if you want to stand out instead of blending in with ho-hum content. You SHOULD if you want an incredible end-product you can *count on* to result in leads, sales, more brand awareness, more authority attached to your name—whatever your goal may be.

And why settle for anything less, my friends?

Invest in Your Team

Developing talent in your team so your business can run without you is an incredible boon. The investment you make in both time and money will pay off when you no longer have to check up on your team constantly or take on all of the important tasks yourself, including writing and publishing content. Instead, once you've delegated, your business will buzz along steadily, growing continuously, with only a few regular nudges and directions from you.

Investing in your team begins with dollars and money. You want your hired talent to be paid *what they deserve,* and nothing less. Otherwise, you risk them jumping ship for a more favorable position with better earnings, and if you have a truly talented person, you don't want that to happen. Hire great people. Pay them well. It will return tenfold to you. Review their pay rates annually and even if they don't ask for more, offer them more if you know what they're worth.

But beyond that, your team investment also involves *investing in the person.* In short, caring for them. Taking time to answer their questions. Taking time to review their work and send kind, detailed critiques, especially if you're the expert hiring them. Understanding when something comes up, and working with them as much as you can. Business owners often underestimate how far this can take them. It's a *must* to build long-term relationships that last for years and return in a happy team giving tenfold talents to you and your business. (But again, you might be too busy "doing it all" that you don't have time for this vital team investment—consider this your red warning flag to hurry up and delegate!)

The Average Budget to Create Great Content

Since delegation is an investment, what should you budget to ensure your content creation stays on track, your creators earn what they deserve, and it all pays off in the form of more traffic, more leads, more trust... more everything?

The median amount full-time content entrepreneurs invest back in their businesses is $10,000, according to research from The Tilt.[15] Additionally, 75% fund their businesses through personal savings. Most don't seek any help from venture capitalists or angel investors.

Of course, "median" means half of all entrepreneurs invest *more* than $10k, and half invest *less.* For me and my businesses, I average a monthly content marketing budget of about $3,000/month, or $36,000/year. That budget is split between writers, a blog editor, a designer, and a video producer.

What YOU budget and invest will depend on a variety of personal/extenuating factors. Before we get into details, let's consider some important data.

First, cost-cutting and skimping on budget are associated with a lack of success. According to Content Marketing Institute's 2021 B2B report, 26% of marketers reported that "internal cost-cutting measures" directly led to their organization's low success with content marketing.[16] Another 63% said "content creation challenges" played a role. Now, that's a broad term, and who knows what it entails, but I'll bet you'll find budget issues underneath that umbrella. To drive that home, 51% of marketers who outsource content said "budget issues" are indeed a top challenge. Usually, this means they can't get enough buy-in from higher-ups to devote to content, or the business is bootstrapped. In more unfortunate cases, they just aren't willing to spend what it takes to make content work, and they don't realize how much it holds them back.

Since we know what entrepreneurs budget and invest, what about small businesses? According to CMI, 57% of small organizations (defined as businesses with anywhere from 1-99 employees) said their budget was less than $100,000. (Only 10% invested more than $100k.) However, the average budget is probably much less, since the median investment for content entrepreneurs is $10k, as we established earlier, and many small businesses are operating with just a few employees. Meanwhile, some 32% of small orgs said they had NO budget at all. (All those content creation challenges and budget issues are starting to make sense. No budget = no plan and no strategy = no good.)

Considering all the data, what should **you** budget for content? Think about:

- The age/financial maturity of your business.

- The number of people you employ and/or outsource to (or the number of people you want to hire to get it done).

- Whether you have established a marketing budget yet, and whether it's working.

- What content metrics you're tracking, if any, and whether you're focusing on the wrong numbers.

- Your goals for your content.

If you're just starting, it's okay to take baby steps and see what works. Set a budget on the low end, then see if it covers all your costs for hiring the right people and creating great content consistently. You can always increase it later, and you'll probably *want to*, but it helps to see it play out in real life and note exactly where each dollar is going and why.

I also recommend focusing on the right metrics to track whether your content is working. Vanity metrics such as likes, shares, retweets, or number of followers do not tell a complete story about how well your content is building trust or converting people into subscribers or buyers. Instead, look at your most important KPIs (key performance indicators) directly connected to revenue, including:

- **Lead generation**: New email subscribers, lead magnet downloads, blog subscribers

- **Brand awareness**: Website traffic, page views, referral links

- **Sales**: People who bought after reading a blog post, people who bought after following your blog for a period of time (your sales rep can collect anecdotes from customers about how they found you—this is super important for understanding how they moved through your content and sales cycle! You can also ask customers this question through a simple survey during checkout.)

Delegation provides a stark contrast to the death-grip so many entrepreneurs and business owners have on the wheel of their enterprises. They feel unable to let go because their business vehicle might veer off into the ditch without their constant supervision—and it probably would, because they never planned and implemented the right delegation process, including the investment needed to make it happen.

If you want to do delegation right, get your mindset right. *Know* you need to invest. *Know* this isn't going to be a one-button wonder where you just click "HIRE" and all your problems go away. *You* need to invest, just as much as you expect your hires to work, write, or build and create for you.

Then *and only then*, you can plan on finding the right partners to delegate to.

How to Find the RIGHT Partners, Build Relationships that Last, & Make Delegation 1000% Easier

Before you can delegate with smart processes—the way that gives you back precious time, the way that keeps your business growing even without you breathing down its metaphorical neck 24/7—**you need to find the right people**.

I cannot say this enough: The. Right. People. Are. ESSENTIAL.

Not only that, but the way you treat them, and the approach you have to the relationship, is also *just* as essential.

Partners>Employees

Find people you can trust, stand back to let them do their best work; and admire and respect them when they show more talent in different ways than you were expecting.

My close-knit team of seven at The Content Hacker are so essential to me. And these high performers, my essentials, are my "partners." Some of them have been my sidekicks on every leading project I've undertaken, closer in the project knowledge and anticipation than my husband, and a part of my world before my first kid was born. *That* is a relationship built to last. These people are not employees. Not contractors. Not even teammates. The people you hire should be side-by-side with you in every step of delegation. They're not working FOR you. They're working WITH you. That means...

...Your partners should deeply understand your goals for your business and whatever part they're involved with—content marketing, management, sales, ecommerce, customer service, etc.

...They should understand your target audience the same way you do.

...They should be experts. In some cases, they should be *as good if not better than you* at completing the tasks you delegate.

And, of course, this goes without saying, but they should be trustworthy, honest, and dependable.

The opposite of all these qualities is exactly what you don't want. There are so many horror stories of entrepreneurs hiring bad apples who create drama or steal time or money from the company, we can amalgamate them into types. Here are the hires you should avoid at all costs, including the red flags to watch out for.

Who NOT to Hire or Partner With

Content Hacker™ / Julia McCoy

Greedy Gary

Who is he? Greedy Gary just wants to take your money and RUN. He may look good for a while (or he may not), and even do some work for you. But in the long run, he's out for one person, and one person only. And that's himself. He has no problem leaving you behind in the dust if profit is ahead, and he might do it on your dime, too.

Red flags: This person often asks for payment up-front, before they deliver any work. They'll also talk a big game and over-promise on what they can do for you (Greedy Gary often crosses over with Overpromising Oliver—see below). If questioned more deeply on their skills, their scam will fall apart, because it'll be clear very quickly that they are NOT skilled. You might see a complete lack of reviews, or one-star reviews buried deep beneath some obviously fake-sounding ones.

I've been scammed by a Greedy Gary. Except his name started with an "E," and he didn't appear greedy at first—instead, the word I would have used was gifted. I'll never forget him. He had real talent, but his greed and desire to "make it big" without any care or regard for the parties involved clouded everything else. We hired him in 2017, discovering him on a freelance platform when we posted a call for editors. He was homeless when we found him, working out of a library; our job was the first source of income he'd had for a few months. He'd been in-between job prospects. Hearing that, I almost got cold feet, but decided to take a chance on him. For a while, it went exceptionally well; he helped us implement some training processes that were brilliant. I wanted to invest in him and show him we were committed to his presence in the team, so, I decided to fly him out for a client's event and comp everything, from meals to hotels to the ticket itself. I sent a second team member with him.

The Sunday they were supposed to be heading back, our second team member present at the event texted me—"Julia, you should know E. is going to quit." *What?* He had full-time editing responsibilities; we were beginning to scale his job duties and rely on him, and I'd just dropped $4k on travel, food and lodging for him to go to an event. I was not happy, to say the least. Plus, to hear this from her, and not E.—strange turn of events! I dialed her number immediately, my hands shaking, and spoke to her. Turns out, E. had gotten starry-eyed at the event and was overheard by our other team member sharing with the key event speakers (who just so happened to also be clients of ours!) that he could assemble a great writing team for them that would cost less than Express Writers and make them millions of revenue, long-term. He told them that he simply wanted a small piece of the pie in exchange for his trouble.

What? Shellshocked, it was all I could say... *huh?* I was thankful my other team member at least knew what was going on, and I immediately began to work to restore the client relationship. I reached out on IM, told the client that E. was no longer on our team, while my husband was removing him from our systems inside the same hour. The client responded, said he and his team had been massively turned off by E.'s behavior, were wondering when he'd be fired, and thanked me for restoring trust in our relationship. They spent over a million dollars on our services in the next twelve months.

One of the biggest red flags with E. was the amount of flattery he bestowed, telling me on every Skype call, every instant message, how honored he was to work with me, how great I was at content, what a majestic leader I was. It felt icky. He also began to profile our other team members and told me he knew their personalities just from the words they typed to each other in Skype. So—multiple red flags. I've been careful to never hire another Greedy Gary since then. You don't want Gary who will greedily backstab you for their own good the first chance they get. Stay far, far away.

Content Hacker™ / Julia McCoy

Slimy Sally

Who is she? Slimy Sally is a copywriter with a sales background who doesn't understand what 21st-century customers want. She was trained and groomed during a time when sales were about in-your-face persuasion and slick techniques instead of gaining trust and building relationships. Today's consumers want to LEARN on their own before they buy—most read 3-5 blogs before ever talking to a sales team![4] Slimy Sally isn't tuned in to what modern consumers want and will turn off your prospects with salesy copy faster than you can say "Cold selling is outdated."

Red flags: A personality mismatch between you and Sally is your first big clue. If you find yourself not jiving with a copywriter or their approach, move on. A Slimy Sally will also have a hard time shutting up because she's so used to the idea of selling someone on a product, idea, or service right NOW—and that applies to selling herself as the ideal hire, too. Finally, don't forget to look at her writing samples and watch out for copy that makes you feel vaguely uncomfortable, turned off, or that reads heavy on the pitch and light on the help.

We stopped working with commission sales reps in 2017 when I noticed that leads were getting *turned off* and emailing me in great displeasure after feeling too pressured to buy after our commission rep pushed them too hard. She had an awesome work ethic, but continually called our clients "big whales," "large fish," "fat wallets," and sadly, it showed in her behavior towards them. Not cool. We made the tough decision to let our commission rep go completely and moved to an hourly client representative role, searching for a person that would talk to our inbound leads and clients with real knowledge, and sell them on our value without being pushy or slimy.

Early 2021, when we had a great person working with our customers from a value-first perspective, not a sales-first approach, we decided to add commission back in to incentivize her. And even then, the majority of her income is earned from salary, not commission. We never wanted to pressure our team to feel they had to chase wallets—instead, it's all about the relationships.

Overpromising Oscar

Who is he? Overpromising Oliver wants to work with you, bad- ly. *Too* badly. He's ready to give you the moon... Or so he says. He may even flatter you. But when it comes time to deliver on something, he'll make excuses, miss deadlines, or ghost you.

Red flags: The Big Promise. This person will assure you, over and over, "I'm an expert in x and y. I've done this thousands of times." You'll notice a lot of talk—make sure to ask for the evidence to back up all that hot air. Ensure they can back up their boasts with proven success and knowledge in the form of testimonials, actual work samples, reviews, references, or some other proof. If they're fairly new in their industry, ask pointed questions about their expertise and pay attention to the answers.

I hear horror stories about entrepreneurs and small biz own- ers duped by an Overpromising Oscar-type (or a Greedy Gary/ Overpromising Oscar hybrid) all the time. One story involves a digital consulting company that was looking out for a client who, ironically, had just been scammed by a developer siphoning money from their website.[5] The consulting company was thus looking for a new developer who could handle rebuilding the client's incredibly complex site.

A group of freelance web developers agreed to take it on, stipulating they must be paid by the hour. They boasted they were experts in Drupal 8, an open-source content management platform the client required. They could complete the work in no time. Everyone agreed to the partnership and stipulations, and signed a contract.

A few months later, the digital consulting company noticed the website rebuild seemed to be going very slowly. They were paying the developers regularly, but not seeing any results. The head of the digital consultants called up the developers to see what was up. The developers reassured her that work was ongoing—the project was just complicated. The head decided to give them the benefit of the doubt.

Time went on, but still, the website seemed to be stagnating. The digital consultant head decided to bring in another developer company to audit the work the *other* developers had completed so far.

What they found wasn't good. The project should have been more than halfway done, and the originally hired developers had barely made any changes. They were barely working—and collecting money they hadn't earned. Six months later, ironically, the web developers took the digital consulting company to court. The company had to hire a lawyer to fight paying bills for hours the developers had not worked.

The two major problems with this partnership? The developers over-promised and, overwhelmingly, under-delivered (if they delivered at all). The consulting company, meanwhile, made the mistake of trusting the developers' project management skills and gave them no incentive to complete the job in a timely fashion.

This story is very common. It also happened to us, almost exactly like the story told above. Except we lost every penny of $60,000 and wouldn't have won a court battle, because the perpetrators were overseas. When I headed Express Writers, early in our development journey we took out a $60k bank loan to pay a development firm up-front to build our ecommerce platform, which to us was worth millions in the long run, but only if it was done correctly. The firm took the money and ran. They never shared any usable code with us.

While it's true that hindsight has 20/20 vision, there are a few things I would have done differently if I could go back. We should have had more calls with the developers to decipher whether there was real knowledge in their team. We should have looked more closely at the initial scope of the project, which didn't represent reality in the end. Ultimately, that "firm" sold us a lie to get our money, and they duped us well. Never again.

As you can see, completely trusting someone who over-promises can get you into a bind. It's even worse when the person you hire is greedy and dishonest, too.

Devious Diane

Content Hacker / Julia McCoy

Who is she? Devious Diane seems like a good hire on the surface. However, she's so crafty, she has duped many biz owners and entrepreneurs into trusting her through surface charm, a fake resume, and quick talking. In reality, she's toxic if not evil, out to cause actual harm and make a buck off of someone else's disaster.

Red flags: You will catch this person in many small lies, which should set off blaring alarm bells. If they're willing to lie about the small, seemingly inconsequential stuff, you can bet they're lying about the big stuff. Watch out if you can't seem to get in touch with any of this person's references or previous employers, or if the "referral" sounds a little too positive and eager to please—it could be a family member staged as Devious Diane's previous employer.

The Devious Diane type comes in many forms. Some may cause problems just for the sheer spite of it. Take one particular tricky employee who worked in an office in Chicago.[6] This lady was not after money or any of the usual targets—she was after your lunch.

Said lunch thief regularly snuck into the basement breakroom and helped herself to a buffet of meals that didn't belong to her. She would methodically take bites out of everything, and whatever she didn't like went in the garbage. When she was done, no lunch was safe, and the other employees would find their midday meals had either disappeared or landed in the trash with one single bite taken out of their sandwiches. The jig was up when one employee discovered his meatloaf sandwich had been devoured. He angrily determined to catch the lunch thief—and he did. Once discovered, she was fired. How did she repay her place of work? By keying everyone's cars in the parking lot.

I don't know whether to laugh... or cry. I can guess what the poor employer did.

When I ran Express Writers, we had our own run-ins with not one, but *three* Devious Dianes. In fact, one of them (who has since passed away from a heart attack), was actually called Diane. *Gasp.*

This story I'm about to tell you is one of the worst I've ever had to live through in my business journey. I've shared snippets with you before in this book, but here is the full, sad tale. This happened back in 2016—notably, my worst failures came right before my greatest successes. (After this epic failure that spun out from hiring three Devious Dianes, I had no place to go but up.

And I did. I showed my detractors what "up" looked like by building a full-fledged content strategy and implementing it to fuel a successful, high-ROI content marketing campaign for the first time! This was one direct factor that led to our leaps from $30k/months to $70k/months, and then ultimately, $100k/per month.

Want more? *Check out my free two-hour class on how to build a sustainable business for the full story: contenthacker.com/freewebinar*

But I digress. The three Devious Dianes were comprised of two sisters (yes, real sisters that lived and worked together) offshore, and one U.S.-based editor I'd hired. Naïvely, I'd trusted the two sisters to completely run my business. After three years of building and earning my trust, the two of them worked in cahoots with the editor to destroy me, my reputation, and take our writers and clients away from Express Writers. In the process, they successfully stole $80k across eight months. They did not have access to client credit cards, the bank account, or anything like that; instead, they artificially inflated their work deliverables and what they were owed, tracking sometimes up to 100x the amount of tasks they'd actually done in one day, adding into their payroll sheet that they'd edited or wrote 40,000 words when it was really 400 words edited. I kick myself, because I was blindly trusting their records without double-checking against work done. (Today, there's not a payroll that goes by that we don't double-check our team's actual work done. Plus, by now, I've learned you can trust your gut about Devious Dianes. Something felt off with them for *months*. I should have followed my gut's prompting sooner.) Before we fired them, we also discovered them sabotaging our content deliverables to clients, inserting horrible statements like a quote from Hitler in a client's blog. Can you imagine how awful this was? (My breath still catches in my throat thinking about it. This is a nightmare, for a content agency owner.)

I had no idea, because I trusted them. They'd spent years building that trust, after all, and their deviousness didn't show itself until year three—that's when they became entitled, stopped treating me with respect, and began to think they could run the business better than me—I know, because that comprised the content of the mass email they sent to all our writers after I fired them. Though my business coach advised me not to, I followed my gut and told all our clients the full truth of what had happened, not mincing any words. We restored *all* our key client relationships and earned more money than we'd ever earned in one weekend after I sent that note out on a Friday night.

Good thing I went with my gut on telling our clients the truth. The very next Monday, these three Devious Dianes proceeded to launch their website and blog, which was a clone of my company's, just mastheaded by a different brand name. Then, from their new domain, they hit up all our clients to try to get them to jump ship. None of them did. Since I'd emailed everyone right away with an apology and bared my soul in that authentic, honest note, we were safe.

Phew! Devious Dianes. Look out for them. That story was hard to put on paper. If you're still reading this far, and you haven't shat your pants, good for you. Great delegation is hard. Avoiding bad eggs, *especially* the devious ones, is crucial.

5 Steps to Finding the Right Partners

As you can tell, finding the right hires and avoiding the horrendous pitfalls makes all the difference. Your partnerships will be 1000% more successful if the people you ultimately choose *from the start* are dependable, honest, communicative, trustworthy. Being good at what they do should come secondary to this.

The bottom line? *Take care* when diving into your first partnership. Do your due diligence and follow these steps.

1. **Trash the Canned/Standard Phone Interview: Actually Test Their Abilities**

Early in our process, we changed our interview to be a real-time test for the open role (writing a sales email if it's a sales role; writing a short blog headline and summary if it's a writing role; etc.). We don't look at resumes. We don't even look at portfolios. We don't care about degrees or academic clout. All we care about? Their on-the-spot writing ability. So, we ask them to write up to 200 words for a real client task if they want the job. (We never use what they produce.)

If you do have to ask questions, don't ask the standard "What strengths will you bring to this position?" or "How do you handle conflict?" These queries will elicit memorized answers that ultimately tell you nothing worthwhile about a candidate. Instead, ask *different* questions. Get creative. Throw a curveball that knocks them off their feet a little. That's when the real person will emerge.

Adam Bryant, writing for The New York Times about "How to Hire the Right Person," recommends throwing in a few interesting questions[8] sure to elicit some real responses that could be more tied to skills:

What kind of animal would you be, and why?

What's the biggest misperception people have about you?

What qualities do your parents have that you like the most?

What is your natural-born strength?

2. Ask for Evidence and Follow Up on It

The person who wants to work with you needs to have evidence they can do the job right and better than anyone else. Ask for a resume, references, or work samples. Go over these materials with a critical eye. If they've provided references or testimonials, check out any names or companies mentioned. Have questions? Keep prodding. Keep asking. And if anything doesn't feel right, *trust your gut.* Your instincts as a creator, business owner, entrepreneur, have been refined by fire. Trust them.

3. Do a Reputation Check

A quick Google search will tell you a lot about a potential hire. And nothing can say a lot, too. Do a few results show up at the top of the page right away for the right person? If so, what are they, and are they positive, negative, or neutral in nature? For example, a result pointing to the person's Facebook page is neutral, unless you dig up any untoward posts on that Facebook page. A result pointing to a recent booking in the county jail, or a Twitter/social feed full of negativity, complaining and hate, is decidedly negative. What if are there hardly any results for their name? That's not good either, if they claim to be great at content creation involving social media. (Not every writer needs a great Twitter feed to be a great writer, though. So, judge this carefully. If you need a social media writer, put "social media presence" higher on the totem pole.)

4. Get Clear on Expectations for Both Sides

Both sides should air their expectations for the job and get clear on them right away—the timeline of the position (temporary, part-time, contract, freelance), major duties, what the pay will be, when it will start, how you'll communicate and interact if the job is remote, and any other details.

Make sure you are 100% upfront about *everything* you are asking for. Don't leave any stone unturned. Then, if you see any hesitancy on their end after expectations are made clear from your end, pause the interview or hiring process until they state everything is clear on their end. For example, one time we had a writer pass our application process. After we sent over the orientation materials, they responded that they *thought* they could commit to deadlines, but kept mentioning they had some event coming up and they weren't sure how it would interfere. The prospective hire never got clear on what that "event" was. I proceeded to set them up with orientation, but it backfired in my face when we gave them work with a deadline, trusted them to deliver, but that unresolved "I have something else to do" came back up, and they never got anything done.

5. Give Them a Trial Period

Sometimes, a person comes off fantastic in interviews but completely fails to live up to expectations while on the job. It's also not unheard of for someone to be gung-ho about a job *in theory*, and even a test interview process, but realize it's not a great fit *in practice*. No one is perfect, and hiring is never a perfect process with perfect results. For this reason, give yourself and your new hire some leeway. A trial period will help you both figure out whether working together is a good fit. It also relieves some of the pressure to impress on both sides.

Stipulate a few weeks or a month for the trial period with check-ins along the way. The right person will be thankful you're making the effort to see if your partnership will work long-term. The wrong person will get weeded out by the process.

Finding good partners isn't easy, but once you have them on your team, you'll be thankful you did the legwork to get them in your corner. With hiring figured out, you'll assemble a team who will help you create amazing content, consistently. *Because content creation is HARD*. Full stop. Getting it right takes more than one person, one day, one stage, or one process.

Need to hire a great content partner? Learn the steps for finding your perfect-fit and my nine must-have traits in a solid content partner: contenthacker.com/how-to-hire-a-writer

Start Delegating: What, When, & How

Here's the secret sauce you should start pouring all over your content marketing *today.*

The what, when, and how of delegation. Or, to put it more gently, letting go of the reins (if that's too hard, just consider it like loosening your grip a little bit—I *promise* it will be okay).

Friend. It's time to hand specific tasks off to people you trust.

Think of this delegation phase as an investment in your growth. This willingness to invest is what will separate you from the tired, overworked content marketers who continually grind to get ahead versus the successful content marketers who don't run themselves ragged.

The latter are rested, growing by leaps and bounds *daily*, energetic, enthusiastic, and in it to win it. It's all due to their willingness to invest in the right content partners. They value their time enough to realize, when they pour their effort into the right places, massive growth will follow.

In the end, that's all delegation does for you. It gives you space and freedom to concentrate your energy where it *really* matters for your business. The smaller pieces come together behind the scenes so you can focus on the big picture.

When it comes down to it, *don't do this content thing alone.* Your marketing, and by extension your business, will be stronger for it.

DON'T Delegate Everything

That said, you shouldn't delegate every single thing. After all, you're the expert practitioner at the helm of your business. Remain in the mix at all times, without doing it all. BE the source of your content ideas, so your rep as an industry force stays indisputably truthful.

***BE the source of your content ideas**, so your rep as an industry force stays indisputably truthful.*

Example: You're invited on a podcast as a guest expert, but you have no idea what you blogged about last week because you completely removed yourself from the mix. You didn't even provide the idea—someone you hired did. Unfortunately, the host asks you live about a point you mentioned on your blog, but you're at a loss because you weren't even involved in the ideation process.

Another example: You're speaking at an event and an attendee asks you to expand on the finer points of a great blog you wrote last month. Same sitch. *Ruh-roh.* You never even researched the topic, so you have no idea what the finer points *are.* You didn't review the blog, either. Your team handled the whole thing without your involvement. Now? You're left gaping like a fish at the event attendee, making up some B.S. that makes you sound amateurish.

See how your reputation starts to crumble a little as each instance adds up?

Reputation *matters* in content marketing. It's what you're trying to build—an authority name for yourself and/or your brand.

Each interaction your audience has with you AND your content has an impact on how that reputation forms. Your involvement in content creation matters for this reason. Don't step out of the process entirely.

This point is more important now than ever. Thanks to the events of 2020, trust is at an all-time critical point.[12] Politically, socially, not to mention health-wise, the world went through the wringer during months of upheaval in all aspects of our daily lives. (Thanks a lot, pandemic.) Overwhelmingly, as Edelman's Trust Barometer shows, consumers lost faith in both the government and the media as information sources. When that happened, they turned to businesses, instead.[13] In 2021, trust in business jumped to 61%, while the government and media sat at trust levels of 53% and 51%, respectively.

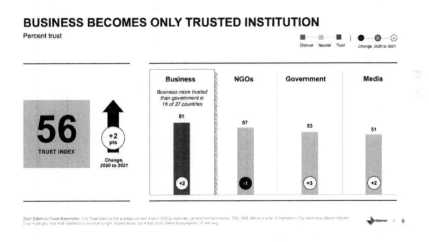

BUSINESS BECOMES ONLY TRUSTED INSTITUTION
Percent trust

Trust is fragile these days. Building it between consumers and your business should be a top priority for you, especially if you want to grow. At this point in history, people are desperate to put their trust *somewhere*, but so many of the options out there seem weak, unsatisfactory, or downright duplicitous. If you can become a trustworthy lighthouse in a stormy sea of shifty, questionable options, that is an incredible differentiator. Don't throw it away.

As you can see, delegation works much like the gears of a finely tuned clock. You must set them in motion correctly, otherwise the time will be off—and even falling behind by a millisecond can ruin the output. On top of that, it's a tightrope act. Delegation requires a fine balance between being involved enough to get the ball rolling steadily, but not so removed that it gets away from you entirely.

Luckily, I've already figured out what you shouldn't delegate vs. what you should for a successful content marketing machine. (Hint: It's exactly how I delegate everything today in my own content operations.)

The Roadmap to Delegation *Or, Why Content Creation Is Not a One-and-Done Process*

When it comes time to begin delegating your content creation process, you may feel lost in space. Where do you begin? Who should you hire first?

A common mistake many people make is over-simplifying content creation and forgetting their strategy. For example, you shouldn't try to squeeze your blog content creation and publishing into a one-and-done stage. It's far more nuanced and complicated than that. And, as I said, it needs space and time to breathe to become something worthwhile (read: something that produces real results for your brand/business).

A common mistake many people make is trying to oversimplify content and create without a strategy.

Let's break down the content creation process into three major stages. The process begins with a kernel of an idea and ends with a polished, optimized, quality content piece you can share everywhere.

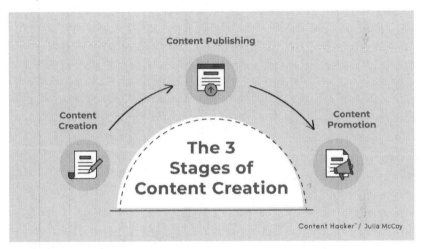

Each major stage involves its own processes and sub-stages. You can certainly modify this as needed. Here's a quick overview of how I break it down, with basic tasks for each stage and sub-stage. *Want deep knowledge of the content strategy and marketing process I use for all of my sustainable businesses? Check out contenthacker.com/transformation.*

The 3 Stages of Content Creation + Suggested Sub-stages & Actions

Content Creation

- Research:

  » Your audience

  » Content topics & keywords

- Ideate:

  » Individual blog topics

  » Outlines of what to cover in each post

  » Both should be based on the preceding research stage

- Write:

  » Write each post, fleshing out the outline, incorporating key-words, and conducting research at each point

- Edit:

  » Proofread and edit each post

- Images:

  » Get custom images made for each content piece: blog header images & CTAs + images correctly sized for social sharing

Content Publishing

- Plan:

  » Plan out when you'll publish blog topics on your content calendar

- Schedule:

  » Schedule posts in advance on your content calendar

  » Draft posts for publishing in advance

- Post:

  » Publish posts based on your content calendar schedule

Content Promotion

- Email:

  » Write a short email to promote your upcoming blog

  » End it with a CTA to the blog post on your site

  » Schedule it to send to your list when the blog goes live

- Social Media:

  » Promote new blog posts and content

  » Develop a presence on the most relevant platforms for your brand

  » Engage with your audience

Keeping the overarching content creation process organized like this is massively helpful. It allows you to:

- Break down content creation, which can seem like a giant task, into smaller, more manageable goals

- Create repeatable processes for each stage and sub-stage, which saves time and maximizes your efficiency

- Organize and schedule content creation, including delegating **who** does **what** and **when**, so it works FOR you rather than against you

If this seems like a lot—well, it is. This is what it takes to create amazing content. Thankfully, you don't have to do it alone. In fact, you shouldn't. *Ever.* And delegating ensures you never have to.

Now that we have an overarching view and understanding of the entire content creation process, let's jump into the major do's and don'ts of delegation.

DON'T Delegate These Tasks

1. The Ideation Process of Each Content Piece

YOU are the expert and the face of your content, so YOU need to be the idea machine.

When all the content ideas come straight from your brain, you'll never worry about how your reputation and your content co-mingle. Instead, it will all be a seamless representation of your particular point of view, expertise, and authority in your industry.

2. Determining Goals for Each Piece

The goals for each of your content pieces may be similar, or they may differ slightly. Either way, they should tie into your larger business goals – which you should have in place at the top of your content plan for the year.

As a general rule, I shoot for at least one of three "goal buckets" with each content piece I publish. Sometimes, I'm able to hit all three at one go. (My content strategy course, *contentstrategy-course.com*, delves much deeper into content marketing goals.)

   a.   Building brand awareness

   b.   Earning sales or connections

   c.   Building SEO rankings

Every single piece of content should be created with a goal in mind. No matter what, your content should work hard for you and help advance your growth. Goals give your content direction, focus, and drive.

As the person most invested in the success of your content, no one should be determining these goals but you.

3. Key Research Points for Each Piece

The key points you use in your content will be the ones you'll reference whenever you draw on your authority.

This is simply a matter of knowing your stuff in your industry. Are you familiar with all the most recent research? The most pressing problems your customers are worried about right now? The new topics your peers are buzzing about? The most frequently asked questions that come up again and again for new customers?

Without a doubt, you'll reference some or all of these topics in your content. Familiarity with them and how/when you addressed them in your content ensures you'll never end up like that out-of-touch podcast guest "expert" with no idea of what they published on their blog last week.

4. Proofreading and Editing Before Publishing

As the name and face stamped on your content, you need to be the last person who touches it. Doing the final proofreading and editing yourself also ensures you stay familiar with the content you publish.

As long as you hire expert writers to take care of the crafting portion, you shouldn't have much editing to do. At most, you'll need to scan the content, check headings and sub-headings, check links, and read a bit from each section.

The key here is making sure you trust the writer you employ to do the heavy lifting. They should specialize in writing for YOUR industry, be familiar with your brand style guidelines, and be intimate with your particular point of view and tone of voice.

This saves you *so much time*, the editing portion should take minutes, so it's not a big deal to do it yourself—especially since it keeps you up to date on the content going out every week (or every month).

5. Adding Personal Stories

Your content writer can write knowledgeably about your industry. Even further, they know how to produce copy that wins both rankings in Google and conversions from readers.

They don't, however, know your personal anecdotes and stories, the pieces that often make your content richer, more relatable, and more engaging.

Where relevant and applicable, add your personal stories to your content yourself while you're in editing mode. (You can't outsource this step, because your writer isn't *you*.)

Think:

- What anecdote would enrich and personalize/humanize X section of your piece?

- What personal story or experience might further illustrate a concept?

- Could you expand on a point your writer made referencing your personal preferences or opinions?

Not all content pieces need your stories, but if you see an opportunity that will make your content richer, go for it.

DO Delegate These Tasks to the Right People

Now that you know what NOT to delegate, it's time to get down to what you SHOULD delegate for smarter content marketing. Happily pass off these tasks to members of your team and pat yourself on the back for working smarter, not harder.

Below, I suggest hiring for these four roles to form your content creation and publishing support team:

1. An expert industry writer

2. A graphic designer/artist

3. A blog editor

4. A social media manager

1. What: Writing the Meat of Your Content Pieces (Post-Ideation)

Who: An expert industry writer

Here's the giant plus about hiring industry writers to craft the meat of your content pieces:

If they're experienced pros, they'll know how to write content that performs well – usually better than what you could produce yourself.

This is especially true if you're crunched for time. Even if writing is your industry, as a brand leader or business owner, you don't have time to produce the type of consistent, quality content you need to get ahead. *Your writers do because it's their entire job.*

That's why I say, **as a general rule, you shouldn't write any of your content yourself.**

Instead, *ideate* what will get written. Then enlist a content writer to help refine your ideas and turn them into published content pieces. Create a thorough outline.

☞ Need an outline template? Check out the outline example in **Chapter 4, Section 2.4** ("Produce a Fully-Formed Topic and Outline [and Write It Down!]"). It's an exact template of what I provide for my writers!

I occasionally write my content, but that's because writing is my expertise. I do it to stay sharp—and because I love it. If you don't have those excuses, you NEVER need to write your content!

2. What: Research (Post-Ideation)

Who: The same expert writer from #1

As your writer crafts your content and fleshes out your ideas, they should naturally use research to support those points. This is a standard requirement for experienced, expert content writers because adding research and links to content is rankings fodder. For many topics, Google loves to see well-researched, well-linked, thorough content pieces that exhaustively expand on a subject.

Adding research to content also provides much-needed context for readers. It's about usability as much as "link juice." Users are looking for signs that you're credible, especially if they need to trust and use the information in your content. Links and citations serve as excellent "credibility signals" because, if included correctly, they should point to related and supporting content for your page. It's all about transparency and staying comprehensive, correct, and current, according to the Nielsen Norman Group, one of the foremost authorities on UX (user experience).[7]

Even for shorter pieces or lighter topics, linking to related authority sources is considered a best practice. Your writer should naturally look for these opportunities and include them because the result will perform better.

This means you shouldn't waste time doing this type of research yourself. Finding stats, facts, studies, and relevant authority sources to support a topic is a writer's job, part and parcel of their work.

That said, if there's specific research you want to mention in a content piece, add a note about it in the brief/outline you give your writer. (More on this later.)

3. What: Image Design, Illustration and Creation

Who: A graphic designer/artist

Sure, you could grab some unedited stock images for your content, slap them on and call it "done," but that won't do anything for your brand image.

The people reading your content (*really* reading it, from top to bottom) will notice the details. Custom illustrated images lend a professional, clean look while also boosting your brand. Not to mention, you'll stand out *much* more from the thousands of other brands slapping said stock images on their blogs and sharing those images on social media.

Beyond stock images, should you D.I.Y. images in, say, Canva? If you throw a cute font on a stock image, does it count as "custom"?

No. Not if you want to grow. And, yes, there's a huge difference between the blog header you D.I.Y. and the header you'll get from a pro graphic designer who customizes your imagery with your branding, colors, and a unique style.

Think of it from this perspective. Did you go to art school? Did you take classes on Photoshop and Illustrator? Did you study composition, color theory, or the principles of good design? Sure, you may have a natural eye for it, but that doesn't equivocate to years of study and practice. If you want share-worthy images that make your brand content stand out, invest in the designer, and delegate this piece of content creation. It will pay off in the long run.

4. What: Scheduling and Optimizing Posts on WordPress

Who: A blog editor

Scheduling and optimizing content are a big deal for rankings and consistency, and a step of the creation process you simply can't skip. So many creators either go lax on this step or jump over it entirely in the name of saving a few dollars, but both roads aren't worth the headaches you'll inevitably encounter.

To earn rankings in search engines, optimization is KEY. This process doesn't end with the writing, either. Once the writing is finished and the draft is transferred to WordPress, there are dozens of tiny actions you can take to optimize your content further. Remember: Content that is not optimized won't rank, even if it's incredible information.

Meanwhile, scheduling helps you stay on top of your content production pipeline. Having posts ready in advance means you'll always keep ahead of your goals, not to mention maintain the consistency that's so necessary to build trust with readers. Luckily, both tasks are great to outsource to a dedicated blog editor who will add the content to WordPress (or whatever content management system you use), optimize it using correct formatting and SEO tactics, and schedule it for publishing.

5. What: Social Media Promotion

Who: A social media manager

Promoting and marketing your content is just as important as creating it. This step will determine how many additional eyes land on your published pieces—or whether you get zero additional traffic or extra leads at all.

Social media is an amazing tool for pulling in new readers and new fans of your brand. But the work that goes into social media promotion is no joke. For the best results, you need to post content *daily* to multiple channels. You need to log into various accounts, post at optimal times, and reshare content. You need to log into your social media tool of choice (Buffer, MeetEdgar, Later) to write and schedule content across your brand profiles to promote events, blog posts, and your products/services. You also need to interact with your followers and respond to DMs. Taken together, all these activities equate to an entire job in and of itself. To build a smarter, leaner business and avoid getting stuck in the weeds, you *must* get help making it all happen.

Your social media manager will do some key jobs for you every single day:

They'll schedule and post blurbs + links to the newest content pieces on your branded accounts (e.g., the ones representing your brand or company as a whole) across Twitter, Instagram, Facebook, etc. – wherever you have a presence.

They'll write and schedule posts across all your branded accounts, using whatever tool you prefer.

They'll post content at optimal times.

They'll engage with your audience on your branded accounts (HUGE for building relationships and trust), including liking posts, commenting, following other accounts, and sharing others' posts.

They **will not** (or they shouldn't) post from your personal profiles (the ones bearing your name). I recommend keeping these in your wheelhouse for authenticity reasons.

Within this sphere of activities, *your* job is to ensure the whole picture—your accounts as single entities—stays consistent and on-brand.

👉 *Note:* The above information is a broad overview of who you should be delegating to within your content creation pipeline. For a deeper breakdown of how each team member fits into the greater scheme of creation, read Chapter 4, **"How to Create Content Without Burnout."**

DO or DON'T Delegate These Tasks (It's Up to You)

The above categories are must-dos to encourage your brand's growth while keeping your authenticity and expert reputation intact.

However, there are some content creation tasks that you can either **delegate or not**. It's totally up to you, depending on your personal preferences and workflow.

1. Research: SEO Keywords

No time to research SEO keywords for your content? Easy: outsource keyword research to a content strategist or SEO-knowledgeable writer. As long as you're coming up with the ideas that will eventually bloom into fully-formed content pieces, a strategist can help you determine the perfect keyword for your suggested topic.

2. Promotion: Writing and Scheduling Blog Promotion Emails

Your email subscriber list needs to know when you just published a new blog or content piece, every single time it happens. You can definitely write these yourself if you have the time/know-how, but it's also totally okay to outsource this work to an expert email writer or blog editor.

SUBJECT

New blog: 64 influential & educational content marketing accounts to follow

PUBLISHED DATE ⊘

October 14, 2021 at 11:51AM

Edit broadcast

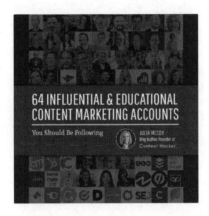

HI [FIRST NAME GOES HERE],

Content marketing is the future. The worth of the industry is about to skyrocket to $600 billion by 2024.

Content marketing generates 3x as many leads as traditional marketing while costing 62% less. The simple truth is, regular advertising methods are inefficient in today's online environment. And organic content geared to pull in leads is working much, much better.

But...

Question. Where or to whom do you go in this industry to learn the ropes?

I also know that real-life experience and observation are the best teachers, and I'd take those learning methods over dry, expensive textbooks any day. (That's why I created courses and workshops to give people the tools they need to build a successful content marketing strategy.)

The good news is that you can start learning for free RIGHT NOW by simply by following top content marketers on social media, and paying attention to what they're doing, saying, and sharing.

My content team & I spent weeks to research and put together today's list. No marketer solicited us for these spots – these are real-life top content marketers and practitioners that have earned their places. Enjoy!

Read today's NEW Content Hacker blog: The Top Content Marketers: 64 Influential & Educational Content Marketing Accounts You Should Be Following

Download the free guide: PDF version of 64 content marketing accounts to follow

- Julia & Team

Content Hacker™

Here's an example of a promotional email I sent for a new blog on The Content Hacker. It's the first few paragraphs of the blog and a link to the blog itself. Simple and effective.

3. Promotion: Writing & Scheduling Social Media Posts Using a Social Media Scheduling App

Much like email writing, if you enjoy writing for social media, by all means, take it on yourself. However, if you would prefer to use that time for other tasks that will grow your brand, hand it off to your social media manager. (I suggest this route, and do it myself, except for the content created for my personal accounts.)

Remember, this applies to your brand accounts, NOT your personal ones. I always recommend keeping those accounts just that: personal and authentic.

Here are a few examples of social media posts written and scheduled by a social media manager on MeetEdgar:

A Facebook post promoting a new blog for Content Hacker.
facebook.com/thecontenthackerbyjuliamccoy

A promotional post that went out on Instagram for The Content Hacker Blog.
@thecontenthacker

Here are a few examples of social media posts I've personally created, at @fementrepreneur. Creating your own social posts is a great way to test new formats, like Reels, or thought leadership statements you dreamed up that your customers/audience will RAVE about.

4. Promotion: Paying to Feature Content (i.e., Facebook Ad Retargeting, Zest.is App, etc.)

Should you delegate your paid promotional tactics? Maybe. It depends on how much you use them—or whether you use them at all.

You could definitely hand this off to a team member in charge of finding opportunities for paid promotion and putting them in place. You shouldn't give that person free rein on this, though, or let them loose with zero guidance on how you want to proceed.

It's probably best to figure out how you want to approach paid promotion, first—including your budget and preferred tools/platforms—lay out a strategy, and then give that roadmap to whoever you're delegating this to.

☞ *Note:* I rarely to never do this. It's just simpler/easier to grow our list, schedule emails with our blogs to our list, nurture them with our new content, and keep creating content that gets ranked and found in Google.

WHEN to Delegate for Maximum ROI

Once you know what to delegate for content creation, when should you start?

The answer is simple: Right away. Start planning NOW. Start delegating NOW.

This means getting a content planning tool in place, one your whole team can access to see what content pieces are on deck, which ones are in production, and the state of any additional content assets.

For my content calendars, I use Airtable. I'm a *big* fan of how great this tool is, and how easy it is to navigate and use for your content planning.

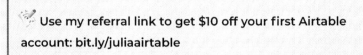

🖊 **Use my referral link to get $10 off your first Airtable account: bit.ly/juliaairtable**

Tabs Explanation:

The Write Blog – Ideation *tab is a brain dump. In no way is this a refined or final tab. Here, I simply record ideas.*

WB – Scheduled Out *tab is where we list finalized pieces written by the writers. I'll also 'brain dump' in the tabs below the pieces I want to come out, but the dates may not be finalized yet. Since my team and I check this tab daily, we won't forget to produce topics we write down here. (i.e., a seasonal Star Wars Day blog that I need to write.)*

WB – Published *is a record of everything published. I double-check this tab and hit Ctrl+F to make sure I'm not duplicating content (a.k.a., cannibalize a keyword). If I am about to duplicate a topic, I simply update that existing topic from the WB – Published record.*

WB Updating Old Content *is a record of all the blogs we update. (We update at least five old blogs per quarter.)*

With this amazing calendar tool, I plan out and schedule blog topics months in advance. The calendar is shared with my designer and blog editor, who assist in adding elements like images, published blog links, and more. Once the ideas are vetted and planned (keywords mapped out, topics created), I assign them to one of my writers – usually months out, so there's plenty of time for them to write/create/edit the piece and send it to me for review.

This also gives my designer plenty of time to create accompanying images for the blog header and social media sharing, as well as any special image requests or infographics to add to the blog content.

My content calendar in Airtable serves as our content marketing hub:

It's a record of all the content I might want to create in the future.

It's a record of all the content I WILL publish and HAVE published.

It tells me **when to delegate**: when to assign a content topic to a writer and when to request image creation from my designer.

It gives me approximate due dates for each content asset.

Your content calendar is also your delegation plan. It's never too early to start planning because the sooner you do, the sooner you can start delegating and getting your content creation machine off the ground.

Delegation Cheat Sheet: WHO to Hire

We've already touched on the experts you need to hire to start delegating content creation, but I'll repeat them here for reference. Here's who you need on your team to make this work:

- **Expert writer(s)** – Paid a fixed, per word rate. I look for content writers and train them up myself as my own personal brand writers.

- **Social media manager** – Paid hourly. You can easily find one by posting a job to Upwork, Indeed, Glassdoor, or LinkedIn.

- **Blog editor/quality assistant** – Paid hourly.

- **Graphic designer** – Produce a ton of visual assets for your content? I recommend hiring an in-house graphic designer. Fiverr is a good resource for low-cost graphic design.

- **SEO keyword strategist/content strategist** – You can hire someone to do ALL your content strategy/keyword research, or you can hire someone for specific topics/blogs. If you don't have your own, consider hiring a freelance strategist.

Chapter 2 Wrap-Up

- Delegation is an action that will revolutionize your content creation process.

- That content you're rushing out the door, that you're struggling to get done all by yourself? It could be so much better. It could bring you *so much more* ROI.

- You need the **right** partners by your side to help bring the incredible content of your dreams to fruition.

- Learn the steps to hire trustworthy people, and avoid these types of hires at all costs:

  » **Greedy Gary** – He's out for no one but himself and his own benefit.

  » **Slimy Sally** – She was raised on outdated sales techniques and writes in-your-face, salesy copy that scares away customers.

  » **Overpromising Oscar** – He makes sweeping promises, but misses deadlines, makes excuses, or ghosts you.

  » **Devious Diane** – She's out to cause drama and mayhem. Steer clear.

- Use the stages and sub-stages of the content creation process to plan how you'll delegate and who you need on your team.

- **DON'T** delegate ideation, goals, key research points in your content, or adding your personal stories. Always be the last set of eyes that reviews your content before publication.

- **DO** delegate the meat of content writing, post-ideation research, image design & creation, social media promotion, and scheduling/optimizing blog posts.

- Always use a content calendar to help you figure out WHEN to delegate WHAT.

- Hire these key people for your baseline team:

  » Expert writer

  » Social media manager

  » Blog editor/quality assistant

  » Graphic designer

  » SEO keyword strategist/content strategist

🔄 **Next up:** Procrastination can kill your creative process, which by extension rings the death knell for your content creation efforts. (Procrastination, by the way, is also a symptom of burnout!) Let's learn how to beat it for good in **Chapter 3**.

Chapter 2 References

1. Institute for Corporate Productivity (i4cp). "You Want It When?" [Press release]. (2007, June 26). https://www.i4cp.com/news/2007/06/26/you-want-it-when

2. Julian Birkinshaw and Jordan Cohen. "Make Time for the Work That Matters." (2013, Sept.) *Harvard Business Review*. https://hbr.org/2013/09/make-time-for-the-work-that-matters

3. Jeff Goins. "How to Get Your Writing Done Every Day: The 3-Bucket System." (n.d.). https://goinswriter.com/three-buckets/

4. Pamela Bump. "The Top 3 Reasons Consumers Read Blogs & How to Attract Them in 2021 [New Data]." (2021, June 4). *HubSpot*. https://blog.hubspot.com/marketing/why-do-people-read-blogs

5. Jennifer Fu. "Horror Stories I: Freelance Developers Gone Bad." (2017, June 14). *Codementor Blog*. https://www.codementor.io/blog/horror-stories-freelance-developers-gone-bad-1dw9mhu8n6

6. Modern HR. "Top 10 Employee Horror Stories." (2016, Sept. 1). https://www.modernhr.com/blog/2016/09/01/top-10-employee-horror-stories/

7. Aurora Harley. "Trustworthiness in Web Design: 4 Credibility Factors." (2016, May 8). *Nielsen Norman Group*. https://www.nngroup.com/articles/trustworthy-design/

8. Adam Bryant. "How to Hire the Right Person." (n.d.). *The New York Times*. https://www.nytimes.com/guides/business/how-to-hire-the-right-person

9. Alice Robb. "The 'flow state': Where creative work thrives." (2019, Feb. 5). *BBC Worklife*. https://www.bbc.com/worklife/article/20190204-how-to-find-your-flow-state-to-be-peak-creative

10. HubSpot. "Not Another State of Marketing Report 2021." (2021). https://www.hubspot.com/state-of-marketing

11. BrightEdge. "Organic Search Improves Ability to Map to Consumer Intent: Organic Channel Share Expands to 53.3% of Traffic." (2019, May). https://videos.brightedge.com/research-report/BrightEdge_ChannelReport2019_FINAL.pdf

12. Julia McCoy. "What Drives Brand Trust Today and Going Forward?" (2020, Dec. 4). *Content Hacker*. https://contenthacker.com/what-drives-brand-trust/

13. Edelman. "Edelman Trust Barometer 2021." (2020, November 18). https://www.edelman.com/trust/2021-trust-barometer

14. Andrew Perrin & Sara Atske. "About three-in-ten U.S. adults say they are 'almost constantly' online." (2021, Mar. 26). *Pew Research Center*. https://www.pewresearch.org/fact-tank/2021/03/26/about-three-in-ten-u-s-adults-say-they-are-almost-constantly-online/

15. The Tilt. "2021 Content Entrepreneur Benchmark Research." (2021, Apr./May). https://www.thetilt.com/research

16. Content Marketing Institute/Marketing Profs. "11th Annual B2B Content Marketing Benchmarks, Budgets, and Trends." (2020, July). https://contentmarketinginstitute.com/wp-content/uploads/2020/09/b2b-2021-research-final.pdf

17. Julia McCoy. "How to Have Lasting Impact: Changing Up Who We Are, How We Serve, and Who We Help With My Upcoming Content Transformation© System." Content Hacker. https://contenthacker.com/how-to-have-lasting-impact/

Chapter 3.
HOW TO BEAT PROCRASTINATION (FINALLY)

"You may delay, but time will not."

– Benjamin Franklin

"Time is an equal opportunity employer. Each human being has exactly the same number of hours and minutes every day. Rich people can't buy more hours. Scientists can't invent new minutes. And you can't save time to spend it on another day. Even so, time is amazingly fair and forgiving. No matter how much time you've wasted in the past, you still have an entire tomorrow."

– Denis Waitley, *motivational speaker & author, The Psychology of Winning*

Many, many guides on the internet would have you believe procrastination isn't that big of a deal.

They'll tell you, cheerfully, to "Get Organized!" To "Make a Schedule!" To "Stop Worrying about Failure!" To "Reward Yourself for Finishing Tasks!"
Sounds easy, right?

As if a smile and a quick little treat will help you defeat the deep, dragging feeling that plagues you when you're exhausted, stressed, *behind*, and failing at your goals. As if a list of the "Top 10 Ways to Stop Procrastinating" will automatically lift you out of that dark hole pulling you dangerously close to depression and burnout.
Ugh. No.

Because, #truth: **Burnout, procrastination, and depression are closely linked.**

It's another tough day at work. A big project is due tomorrow, one you've been putting off for weeks. Now you have 24 hours to get it done, and you're panicking. After spending a frantic day putting all the pieces together for the presentation, you still need to finish the accompanying report. You work late, typing bleary-eyed behind your computer at 9:30 p.m., when you add that final period to the last sentence.

When you cross the threshold of your home, you realize, too late, that you forgot to eat dinner. You rummage in the cupboards and come up with a bag of chips and a dusty apple you can't remember ever buying. A can of sugary, caffeinated soda rounds out your three-course meal. You collapse on the couch and zone out on Netflix for hours. Oops.

The next day, you have an early start—you need to prepare for your presentation, but you wake up too late to even shower before work. You feel like a zombie and look like one, too, with dark bags under eyes that are red-rimmed and bloodshot. You slam a double espresso just to get through the morning, then chug two Red Bulls at lunch to fight the afternoon drag until your Big Meeting.

It's time for your presentation. While you look like a zombie, you feel like Death, even though it would be impossible for Death to have a massive ball of anxiety rolling around in the pit of its stomach. As you walk into the meeting you know, with a sinking feeling, you did not prepare well enough for this.

Your self-fulfilling prophecy comes true. Your customary creativity, verve, and fantastic ideas are M.I.A. during your PowerPoint. To put it lightly, you flub it. You mix up your notes. One important slide is missing from your deck that you totally forgot. Your report is riddled with grammatical errors and outdated facts you meant to update but didn't. During the question-and-answer session, your mind goes blank and you stammer awkwardly instead of providing confident replies.

When the Hour of Horror is over, you slink back to your office in shame. This was a chance to show off your prowess. Instead, you made everyone question your position and your business. After this ultra-failure, you can't bring yourself to get going on any other projects looming on the horizon. You feel worse than you did yesterday, and the day before—a slow progression into the hole you now wouldn't mind crawling into. Though you have tasks to complete—content to write for your blog, meetings to set up, emails to write—you quit for the day two hours early and go home to more Netflix and junk food. And the cycle starts all over again.

The above scenario is sad, and yet, too common. Worst of all, some people don't even realize they're drowning because the loop of procrastination to burnout to depression is insidious. It can creep up on you despite yourself. And the outside world does not help us avoid the loop—if anything, society and the internet and social media and our peers make it worse, especially if we start relying on them too much.

What's worse than those falsely cheerful online guides telling you, in effect, to "just get over it"?

Googling how to overcome procrastination in a desperate, last-ditch effort to make some kind of change in your life, and Google giving you downright *horrible information* right off the starting block.

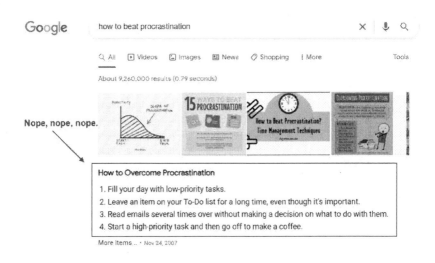

This is what you'll find on Google's SERP (search engine results page) for "how to beat procrastination". Go ahead. Follow the tips listed in that first Featured Snippet. That won't lead to disaster, surely. Am I pouring on the sarcasm thick enough?

"Start a high-priority task and then go off to make coffee"? "Leave an item on your To-Do list for a long time, even though it's important"? It's almost funny, this advice is so bad. (Almost.) This is obviously a case of Google's crawlers snagging the wrong information to populate a Featured Snippet. At the same time, this is a prime example of how even Google can't save you if you're deep in the procrastination-burnout-depression cycle.

Google is far from having all the answers all the time. So, who or what should we rely on? How do we get *out* of this disastrous loop? How do we stop sabotaging ourselves? Our content marketing? Our businesses?
Our livelihoods?

Here's the problem.

When you're not reaching your goals...

...When you're behind on your content calendar, when you have days and weeks piling up where you're not posting anything, when what you DO post is crap that gets zero traction, results, leads...

...When you're messing up important projects and deadlines...

...When your business is floundering because you're not growing, and you can't seem to get out of the red or make any headway...

...When you're relying on outside factors to pull you through pro-crastination, when you focus on the wrong things to save your-self...

Procrastination becomes dire. It becomes a symptom of a larger problem. And if you keep doing it, your dream WILL die.

Procrastination *cannot* be overcome with a few positive affir-mations and a handful of throwaway tips sprinkled on top. You *cannot* beat this with some determined googling. Nor can you conquer it by ignoring it. No—it takes mental work to get out of the burned-out, procrastinating, depressed loop you're stuck in.

Only then can you get on the right path to creating content without batting an eyelash, without burnout, without putting off important tasks until it's too late. And, once you're in a good, healthy place where you're not stressing, constantly worrying, behind, late, spiraling...

You'll grow. And so will your business.

That's why I included this too-important chapter in this book. It's a vital piece every content creator NEEDS in their wheelhouse if they want to succeed. What I'm about to share is how I per-sonally beat procrastination, along with the demons that come with it.

What Science Says About Procrastination and What Causes It

Beating procrastination is all about understanding its root cause. Because procrastination doesn't just materialize one day to plague your work and your life. It doesn't show up without rhyme or reason. **Procrastination happens because specific psychological factors are at work.** Thus, understanding these factors gives you some powerful tools to banish procrastination from your life.

Before we go any further, let's get something straight. Procrastination has zero to do with your self-control. It has nothing to do with laziness. You don't procrastinate because you're a slacker. And you certainly don't do it because you're flawed.

You procrastinate because the mental reward for putting off a task is available to you *right now.* In comparison, the reward of completing the task and getting it off your plate will only happen at some indeterminate time in the future. The promise of the immediate reward versus the future reward is too tempting for SO many of us. For instance, you dread working on that report because it's really tough to write. You subconsciously want to avoid the mental anguish it will cause you to write it, so you put it off. BAM. Relief floods your brain because, now, you don't have to worry about the report until later. No matter that eventually finishing will give you a better reward and a bigger rush of endorphins. The fact that one reward is available right NOW makes it more tempting and more important—even though it's a *lesser* reward.

In other words, you procrastinate because you get to put off the discomfort, frustration, anxiety, boredom, difficulty, or any other negative emotion completing the task at hand causes you. That gives you an immediate sense of relief.

Researchers have previously linked this type of "short-term mood repair" and procrastination. Particularly, a study[2] examined how procrastination represents a disconnect between our future selves and our current selves. Here's how the study authors, Dr. Fuschia M. Sirois and Dr. Timothy A. Pychyl, put it:

*"We believe that tomorrow will be different. We believe that **we** will be different tomorrow; but in doing so, we prioritize our current mood over the consequences of our inaction for our future self."*

Our future self. That's a person we don't know. That's a person we don't have to worry about now, right? Maybe that's why we have no problem dumping the negative consequences of procrastination straight on our poor, tired future shoulders.

Describing procrastination as "mood repair" also neatly links it back to depression. In many ways, procrastinating becomes a coping mechanism for people who are depressed—clinically or otherwise.[3] Some of the key symptoms of depression are a lack of interest in nearly all normal activities, tiredness and low energy, and trouble concentrating,[4] all of which can make completing even mundane tasks next to impossible. Procrastination gives you an excuse as to why you can't seem to get anything done, and also provides a sort of short-term relief. "*I'm so tired. I'll just get this done next week. Now I can at least relax for a while.*"

By the way, that's exactly how procrastination snowballs. Procrastinate too much, and you'll be left drowning in tasks your past self put off for another day. Because, eventually, that future day does come, and you'll crash under the weight of what you tried to avoid days, weeks, or months ago.

What Makes Procrastination Worse?

Since procrastination is a coping method, we can surmise that certain actions and habits will exacerbate how much we procrastinate and when. These habits make life harder for us in general. They take a toll on our bodies and minds, contributing to depression, burnout, and stress, not to mention heightening our predilection for developing various illnesses and diseases.

1. Not Getting Enough Sleep

You've heard this one over and over. Good sleep is crucial for good health. But did you know it's also essential for good **mental health**? The sleep you get—both the amount and the quality of rest—has a major impact on your mood and mental clarity as well as how your brain functions and how it acquires and remembers new information. For example, while you sleep, your brain "replays" new information you learned during the day to strengthen and consolidate it.[6]

Losing sleep can also make you more prone to physical illness, because, during sleep, our immune system ramps up and performs critical functions it does not do while we're awake. According to a 2012 study[5] on sleep and immune function,

"...Research ... has accumulated surprisingly strong evidence that **sleep enhances immune defense, in agreement with the popular wisdom that 'sleep helps healing'.**"

This is why, at a base level, you need to focus on getting the sleep you need. Lack of sleep can cause a ripple effect that will touch every aspect of your daily life, and the negative results can and will spiral out of control if you keep it up, exacerbating and heightening mental problems you may already be prone to through genes or personality.

Once sleep deprivation is part of our daily lives, enter feeling crappy 24/7. Enter fatigue. Enter burnout. Enter procrastination, failure, depression.

Bottom line: Fix your sleep so you at least can function during your day-to-day. This will strengthen your body and mind so you can face the bigger issues at play.

2. Too Much Caffeine

Eek. This one's hard to hear, for us coffee lovers, but it's the truth. Sleep deprivation and too much caffeine go hand-in-hand. Didn't get your 40 winks last night? Down the coffee and energy drinks the next day to pull through. We Americans love our caffeine, particularly. We're some of the biggest coffee consumers in the world, with each of us guzzling an average of about 3.1 cups per day. 62% of us drink it daily, and 7 in 10 drink it weekly.[7] Does everybody just really love coffee or are we all sleep-deprived zombies looking for our next caffeine hit? I think it might be a little bit of both. I, for one, love my morning cup as much as the next person, but for me, the key is moderation. Here's why.

Over-caffeinating can hurt your mental and physical health. It makes you irritable and twitchy. It can heighten your anxiety or nervousness. It can cause your heart to beat faster. It can give you headaches. It can give you heartburn. It can over-stimulate your brain (if you've ever been wired after too much coffee, you know this distinctly unpleasant feeling—like your head is disconnected from your body). Long term, the effects are more serious. Too much caffeine regularly can lead to osteoporosis (brittle bones), fertility and pregnancy issues (like miscarriages), gut issues, and increased blood pressure.

Coffee isn't the sole culprit or the sole way to get your caffeine shot, however. 80% of U.S. adults take in some form of caffeine daily, not just coffee.[8] Don't forget about caffeinated sodas, energy drinks, teas, espresso, and chocolate.

Whatever way you get your caffeine fix, it's easy to see how it can worsen your mental state and make procrastination more likely. Imagine: You didn't get enough sleep last night, so you need more coffee to stay awake and alert during the day. You have a big meeting you feel nervous about, and all the caffeine makes it worse. You're jumpy and your heart is racing. During the meeting, you can't think straight, so when it's your turn to talk, you're not as convincing or as self-assured as you hoped you'd be. When the meeting is over, you feel defeated. That "I failed" feeling follows you around all day. Later, you can't fall asleep because you keep ruminating on what went wrong. The next morning, the cycle repeats.

Now, I'm not saying you should give up your daily cup of coffee or tea. I'm saying don't let caffeine become a crutch for you. Don't use it to prop yourself up. Don't use it as a coping mechanism when the fall-out from your other bad habits catches up and crashes down around you. **When you overdo it, it can and will make everything worse**. SO not worth it.

3. Not Eating Enough Healthy and Clean Foods

If your diet mainly consists of unhealthy or processed foods, you're setting yourself at a disadvantage from the get-go. All those foods provide, at the bare minimum, is energy. Calories. Nothing else. No vitamins, no minerals, and nothing that helps your body's numerous complex processes function better. If you feed your body garbage, then your body will perform like garbage. And no, I'm not talking about athletic performance. I'm talking about the daily performance your body carries out hour by hour, minute by minute, *to keep you alive*.

It's no wonder so many of us are struggling. We're functioning without the fuel we need to do our best, to live our best lives. No sleep, too much caffeine, junk for breakfast, lunch, and dinner— it should be no surprise when we end up spiraling into procrastination, burnout, and depression. Our bodies and minds are starving for nourishment. How are we supposed to survive life's hurdles and thrive when we don't have the energy, mental clarity, or strength to do it?

The link between depression and the quality of your diet has been studied before. In 2015, researchers found that people who ate a typical Western diet—processed foods, lots of sugar, salt, and fat—had a smaller hippocampus, the part of the brain associated with memory, learning, and mental health.[9]

What happens when the hippocampus shrinks? To put it simply, cognitive decline, which includes our memory, emotions, problem-solving, judgment, and more. Healthy eating is not just about staying fit or losing weight. It's about giving your body what it needs to function mentally and physically so you can live your best life.

4. Not Moving Your Body

We all know, as humans, we need to exercise to keep our bodies healthy. But what about our minds? Yep, exercise (or a lack thereof) affects that, too. If you're not moving in *some* way regularly, if you sit in a chair for eight hours a day at work, then go home and sit for another five hours on your couch watching TV, you're putting yourself at risk physically AND mentally. You'll be much more likely to develop dementia, stroke, heart disease, diabetes, and, *yes*, depression.

Did you know exercising can be just as effective as medication at treating depression? It's true—research has shown that moving your body causes the release of proteins called "growth factors" that make your nerve cells grow and form new connections.[10] This improves brain function, which in turn helps alleviate depression. Coincidentally, this nerve cell growth supports the growth of your hippocampus, which, as we talked about, has a huge impact on how you feel, your mental state, your productivity, and so much more.

I get it—so many of us deeply dread exercise. But it doesn't have to be a giant commitment. And you *don't* have to be an athlete to enjoy it. Do talking walks in nature energize you? Go more often! Do you love doing cannonballs at the community pool? More power to you. Do you feel centered and at your best when you wake up with the sun for a refreshing yoga flow? It all counts.

You don't have to train like an Olympian or even have a muscled body to enjoy exercise and get all the benefits. So, it's time to get out of that rut and find the movement that feels good to you, that comes naturally, that you enjoy. Your mind and body will thank you.

5. Not Challenging Your Creativity, Problem-Solving, & Imagination

This last bad habit can have a potentially deep impact on your brain health. Long-term, it could heighten your risk for developing dementia and Alzheimer's disease.[11] Short-term, it short-changes you in terms of building up skills that could help you cope better with tough situations in all aspects of your life. (Read: burnout, procrastination, depression.) It also may rob you of a lot of joy.

It's failing to challenge yourself mentally. And, no, I'm not talking about stressful work challenges, like when you're finishing that white paper in the wee hours of the night when it's due tomorrow. I'm not talking about the mental challenges you face daily, like figuring out what to cook for dinner or how you're going to juggle your schedule.

I'm talking about challenges that stretch your creativity and imagination in a relaxed, fun setting. Research has shown that these types of "work," ones that combine play with a challenge, are the most optimal types for building creativity.[12] And, you NEED creativity if you want to be successful wherever you are.

By the way, creativity is a **whole-brain** process.[12] It's a total myth that creative people are traditionally "right-brained" and non-creative people are "left-brained." And, saying people are either creative or not is also false. **Everyone, no matter who they are, no matter their education, background, job, or status, can be creative**. Creativity is a skill you can build! It's also not limited to traditional outlets like drawing, painting, or designing. Creativity is a multi-faceted ability that can be used in infinite ways. When you brainstorm a new idea for how to solve a problem on the job, that's creativity at work. When you express yourself through words, photos, makeup, fashion, or how you decorate your office, that's creativity. When you discover a better or faster way to complete a task, boom. There it is again. Your innate, unique creativity will start popping up everywhere if you pay attention.

That's why, in the face of a creative quandary, it's so sad when you throw up your hands, say, "I'm just not creative," and give up. *You could be*. If only you knew it's possible to build your skill with a little fun, challenging mental play.

For instance, if you've never played an instrument, why not pick one up and try to teach yourself with YouTube videos, or by signing up for lessons? The same goes for other fun skills you can learn in your spare time—cooking, baking, photography, knitting, painting, gardening, pottery, yoga, swimming, weight-lifting, even coding websites—as long as it's a new skill that intrigues you, and you have fun learning it, it's a great way to flex your creativity. Don't forget the smaller ways to build creativity, either. Pick up a book and read a few pages every night before bed (reading is one of the BEST ways to challenge and stimulate your mind). Do a crossword puzzle with your morning coffee. Invite your friends over and play an immersive board game.

Just don't neglect your creative muscle. It will come in handy in all aspects of your work and life, and may be the lynchpin that helps you work your way out of a mental struggle like procrastination.

Do the Work: Cultivate These Practices to Slay Procrastination

How do you get out from under procrastination, depression, and burnout? You need to stop the cycle in its tracks. The only way to do that? Through building good habits.

Take it from me. Building good, healthy, constructive, positive habits simultaneously builds better mental health. Better coping mechanisms. A better mindset about your life and how to live it so you feel fulfilled and resilient in the face of whatever hurdle is facing you down today, tomorrow, or in the future. My knowledge here is deep because I've been through it.

In fact, because this topic is *so* important to me, I teach a course solving this very problem, The Mindfulness for Creators Course. Sidenote: it *doesn't* include your typical and general hacks, but mindset, setting and nutrition practices I've honed after ten years of working on my own mental and physical health. Learn more about it at **contenthacker.com/mindfulness.**

1. Start Shaping Healthier Habits Through Daily Practice

As we explored in Chapter 1, habits are *not* built in a day. You can't do a few healthy activities once or twice and expect them to stick for good.

Repetition is KEY, and your secret to good habit stickiness. So is not overloading yourself. Start with one new, good habit you can implement right now. Do it as often as possible. Keep at it, even when you don't feel like it. After a certain amount of time, it will start feeling less like work and more like second nature.

This concept is proven in science. According to health psychology researchers at University College London, it takes over two months—66 days—for a new habit or behavior to become automatic.[13] And that's if you're dedicated. For many people, it takes even longer. In the study, some people spent as long as 254 days making their new habits stick.

This isn't meant to be discouraging, but heartening. Everyone stumbles on the road to building new habits. It might take a long time before it's automatic and easy, but what matters more is *the act of doing.* Don't focus on long-term success, but rather day-by-day wins. As long as you keep it up as often as you can, you'll reap the benefits.

Experts Chime in: Mark Schaefer, Schaefer Marketing Solutions – *businessesgrow.com*

Even your content marketing can become a good habit! *Mark Schaefer*, veteran content marketer and founder of one of the top five business blogs in the world, shares how to turn content creation into a positive habit with four disciplines:

I blogged 650 weeks in a row. I've had my Marketing Companion podcast for nine years without missing an episode. I've written nine books. And many people wonder how in the world I can do this so consistently. Creating content is a matter of discipline ... four disciplines, in fact.

First, you must be aware of the story ideas everywhere around you. You're bombarded with hundreds of interesting ideas and messages every day. View the whole world as a story machine. Look at news stories, ads, graphs, photos, movies, speeches, videos, and questions from colleagues as a perpetual idea engine. Here is your lens: "How is this a potential story for my audience?"

Next, write your ideas down! Use a notepad, your smartphone, or a napkin, but capture your ideas before they are lost!

The third discipline is to schedule sacred time to create content. If creating content is a priority, you should schedule time for it, just like you would for working out at the gym or attending a business meeting. Even an hour or two each week can produce great results.

Finally, you must be relaxed. It's hard to be creative with the stress of a daily life all around you. Find a space and time where you are calm and distraction-free.

If you follow these disciplines, you'll never have to face an in-timidating blank screen again. When it's creating time, simply choose the most fun idea you captured that week and begin to produce your awesome content!

3. Practice Mindfulness

How do you feel when you're on the verge of procrastinating? Tired? Stressed? Anxious? As we've discussed, procrastination is a coping mechanism that helps us push away the negative feelings we get when faced with some kind of hard task. Putting off the task puts off the feelings, and we get immediate relief.

What if, instead of avoiding those feelings, you let yourself feel them? What if they're neither good or bad—they're just *happening*?

The practice of mindfulness is all about being present in your mind and body, noticing what you feel without judgment, and letting it pass. Eventually, the goal is to clear your mind and just *be* for a few minutes. Let your body relax, breathe. When your mindfulness session is over, you should feel calmer, more grounded. You'll feel looser, less tense, and less stressed.

You can see why mindfulness may be helpful for those of us who struggle with our mental health and productivity. In many ways, procrastinating is a symptom that tells us we're waaay too far inside our own heads. Mindfulness lets us step back, distance ourselves from our emotions and the situation, and return to it with calm and focus. Consider it another tool to add to your arsenal, one that may help you break out of the procrastination-burnout-depression cycle.

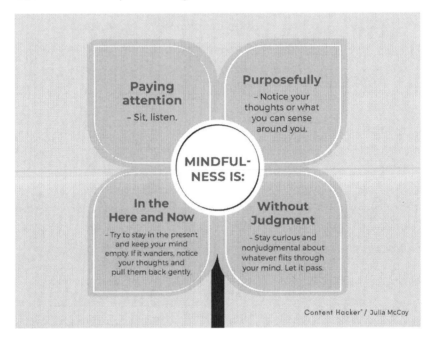

Content Hacker® / Julia McCoy

Mindfulness is:

Paying attention – Sit, listen.

Purposefully – Notice your thoughts or what you can sense around you.

In the Here and Now – Try to stay in the present and keep your mind empty. If it wanders, notice your thoughts and pull them back gently.

Without Judgment – Stay curious and nonjudgmental about whatever flits through your mind. Let it pass.

4. Set Solid Boundaries to Avoid Burnout

When you're burned out, you're overloaded. The tank is empty. You have too much weight on your shoulders and you no longer have the energy to tackle any of it. In short, you're expecting too much of yourself when you have nothing left to give.

Let me make this very clear. You CANNOT do everything. You CANNOT say yes to everyone. It's physically impossible. If you try, you'll end up buried. That's why it's so important to set clear boundaries for yourself.

For example: If you work from home, choose a cut-off time for when you'll close your computer and stop working. Do not compromise it. Set it in stone.

We've all been there. You have SO much work to do. You get in busy mode. 5 p.m. rolls around, then 6, then 7... and by the time you finally stop, you realize you're bleary-eyed, exhausted, hangry, and ready to throw your computer out the window. Friends, repeat this scenario, and you're headed on the fast-track straight to burnout. Not worth it.

Instead, set a boundary for how late you'll work each day. When you KNOW your cut-off time is 5 p.m., you'll try harder to keep it sacred. You'll work more efficiently because you won't have those spare hours dangling at the end of the day to "finish things up."

If you're a workaholic, make it harder for yourself to dive back in. Shut down your computer. If you can, leave it in another room and close the door. Turn off your notifications and set your phone to silent mode. Set up an email responder that tells people you'll get back to them the following morning.

You can't work 24/7 and not expect to burn out. You *must* give yourself some space to recharge. You are not a machine, you're a living, breathing human who needs rest and care. Set those boundaries between work and your personal life, and give your batteries a chance to recharge. You'll perform better—trust me.

5. When Stuff Gets Hard, Don't Give Up!

When we're in the thick of the procrastination-burnout-depression cycle, it can feel easier to just give up on what we thought we wanted, or on opportunities we're struggling to handle. But, I exhort you—please, please don't give up. The very thing you're struggling with right now could be the lifeline that saves you.

Bad habits can mess with our brains and bodies and take away our ability to see the bigger picture. But that larger image is what you NEED to see. It's the overarching goal we lost sight of. It's the completed project that will advance our business. It's the content marketing strategy that will fuel our growth.

When you feel like you want to give up, pause instead. Zoom out. Remember you're only looking at random puzzle pieces right now. Eventually, they will combine to create a beautiful picture. But you must persevere to make that happen.

In my journey with Express Writers, there were countless times when I was burned out and on the verge of giving up. But I didn't. I powered through countless struggles to end up here—past year 10 in business, successfully exiting with a million-dollar deal.

You can't wait for good feelings to magically show up. You have to create them yourself, through the habits you practice every single day. Shape (and reshape) your life. Give yourself the tools to get through any setback, any struggle. Ask for help if you need it. The only way out is *through*.

Experts Chime in: Craig Cannings, Freelance University – *freelanceu.com*

As we close out this chapter, let's turn to some parting words of wisdom from *Craig Cannings*, the co-founder and Chief Learning Officer of Freelance University—an educational community specifically for freelancers to level up their skills. Craig has been freelancing since 2003, so he has some great advice that meshes beautifully with what we've discussed in this chapter:

It's inevitable that successful entrepreneurs at one point or another will push themselves close to, or even beyond, their "breaking point." There is always so much to get done that it is an elusive trap to prioritize your business results over your personal health and important relationships. In my life, I need regular "signposts" to keep me on track so I avoid entrepreneurial burnout.

Here are four signposts to help to steer your business and life in a healthy and meaningful direction.

1. My Big Why

There is a great proverb that says, "Without vision, people will perish." I believe that a BIG WHY can provide a clear vision and even function as a "light in the storm" when things aren't going well! My WHY is an anchor that helps keep my priorities in check so that I don't place work over family, success over integrity, and results over relationships.

2. My Community

"It takes a village to raise a great entrepreneur." Isn't that the truth? It's so critical to have people in your life who champion you and your business, whether they're a spouse, friend, or mentor. You need people walking the entrepreneurial journey with you and keeping you in check when burnout is on the horizon. Make sure to listen intently to the people who care most about you!

3. My Self Care

As you know, a flight attendant on an airplane will always tell you to put your oxygen mask on first before you help the person next to you. This is a terrific principle to live by. If we do NOT take care of ourselves first, then we will ultimately be no good to our business and the people we serve. Build in regular rituals that offer rest and recovery from your busy life such as exercise, quality time with family and friends, volunteering, prayer and other hobbies.

4. My Productivity

As a busy entrepreneur, it is critical to put productivity practices in place that will allow you to get more stuff done in less time. You might time-block or batch your common weekly activities, check your email only twice a day, or do work hustles no longer than 60 minutes before taking a break. At the end of the day, a hyper-productive entrepreneur will add margin to their life and have the freedom to invest in the things and people that truly matter!

Chapter 3 Wrap-Up

- Procrastination happens NOT because you're lazy, but because specific psychological factors are at work.

- Procrastination, at its base level, is mood repair. It's a symptom of a larger problem.

  » The task(s) we face make us feel uncomfortable or distressing feelings. We avoid the task(s). BOOM. We feel better.

- What makes procrastination worse? Bad habits that impair our mental and physical health, and thus our ability to cope:

  » Losing sleep

  » Too much caffeine

  » An unhealthy diet

  » Staying physically inactive

  » Staying mentally inactive off the clock

- What can we do to banish the procrastination-burnout-depression cycle? Build good habits, ones that help us cope with tough situations and get through them.

  » Choose a good habit, practice it as often as possible until it's automatic. Repeat.

  » When faced with the procrastination symptom, face what you're *actually* feeling through mindfulness.

  » Set boundaries and slow down so you're not driving 100 mph on the road to burnout.

» Don't give up. Ask for help, work on good habits, and work on creating good feelings. They won't come without effort. But the effort is worth it.

Next up: Ready to learn all the techniques, tips, and tricks to create content without burnout? I share everything I know about creating content the smart way for websites, your blog, your email list, and YouTube in **Chapter 4**.

Chapter 3 References

1. https://google.com/search?q=how+to+beat+procrastination. Retrieved on July 12, 2021.

2. Fuschia M. Sirois, Ph.D, & Timothy A. Pychyl. "Procrastination and the priority of short-term mood regulation: Consequences for the future self." (2013). *Social and Personality Psychology Compass*. https://doi.org/10.1111/spc3.12011

3. Vanessa Caceres. "When Is Procrastination a Matter of Mental Health?" (2021, May 14). *U.S. News*. https://health.usnews.com/wellness/articles/is-your-chronic-procrastination-actually-a-matter-of-mental-health

4. Mayo Clinic. "Depression (major depressive disorder)." https://www.mayoclinic.org/diseases-conditions/depression/symptoms-causes/syc-20356007

5. Luciana Besedovsky, Tanja Lange, & Jan Born. "Sleep and immune function." (2012). *Pflugers Archiv*. https://www.ncbi.nlm.nih.gov/pmc/articles/PMC3256323/

6. Björn Rasch & Jan Born. "About Sleep's Role in Memory." (2013, Apr.). *Physiological Reviews*. https://www.ncbi.nlm.nih.gov/pmc/articles/PMC3768102/

7. National Coffee Association. "NCA releases Altas of American Coffee." (2020, Mar. 26). https://www.ncausa.org/Newsroom/NCA-releases-Atlas-of-American-Coffee

8. Healthline. "The Effects of Caffeine on Your Body." (2018, Sept. 28). https://www.healthline.com/health/caffeine-effects-on-body

9. Felice N. Jacka, Nicolas Cherbuin, Kaarin J. Anstey, Perminder Sachdev & Peter Butterworth. "Western diet is associated with a smaller hippocampus: a longitudinal investigation." (2015, Sept. 8). *BMC Medicine*. https://doi.org/10.1186/s12916-015-0461-x

10. Harvard Health Publishing. "Exercise is an all-natural treatment to fight depression." (2021, Feb. 2). *Harvard Medical School*. https://www.health.harvard.edu/mind-and-mood/exercise-is-an-all-natural-treatment-to-fight-depression

11. Alzheimer's Society (U.K.). "Risk factors for dementia." (2016, Apr.) https://www.alzheimers.org.uk/sites/default/files/pdf/factsheet_risk_factors_for_dementia.pdf

12. Scott Barry Kaufman & Carolyn Gregoire. "Ten Habits of Highly Creative People." (2016, Jan. 20). *Greater Good Magazine*. https://greatergood.berkeley.edu/article/item/ten_habits_of_highly_creative_people

13. Phillippa Lally, Cornelia H. M. van Jaarsveld, Henry W. W. Potts, & Jane Wardle. "How are habits formed: Modelling habit formation in the real world." (2009, July 16). *European Journal of Social Psychology*. https://doi.org/10.1002/ejsp.674

Chapter 4.
TECHNIQUES: HOW TO CREATE CONTENT WITHOUT BURNOUT FOR...

"Content marketing is the marketing and business process for creating and distributing content to attract, acquire, and engage a clearly defined and understood target audience—with the objective of driving profitable customer action."

Joe Pulizzi, *Epic Content Marketing: How to Tell a Different Story, Break through the Clutter, and Win More Customers by Marketing Less*

Congratulations: The work we've done up to this point has been mostly mental, not physical. *You got through it.*

That's because, to get to a place where you can create content without burnout, you needed to first reset and reframe your mindset about what it takes. As it turns out, becoming an efficient, productive, smart, successful creator is not just about process or knowledge. It's also about beliefs. Habits. Investment. Mental strength. Flexibility. Boundaries. Resilience.

If you're still in the painful process of making a shift to get your mind right, keep going! It's hard work, but it's worthy work with an incredible payoff if you can stick it out. If you're further along the path and feeling excited to learn practical steps, I'm raring to share them with you. It's GO TIME.

Now that you've shifted the way you think about and approach content creation—tackling it in stages versus facing one giant mountain of a task, delegating key parts of the process, fixing your procrastination—we can move on to the nitty-gritty act of getting your content out.

"Is there a process I can follow?"

Yes, my friends. (Let's all breathe a collective sigh of relief. You *don't* have to reinvent the wheel every time you want to create content.) For every single piece of content you want to push out into the world, there's a process you can follow—a repeatable, step-by-step plan you can use over and over again to create, publish, and promote it.

This process uses your brainpower plus the super talents of the team you assemble and delegate to, plus a few handy tools. It also follows the stages (Creation, Publishing, Promotion) and sub-stages (Research, Ideate, Write, Edit) we laid out in Chapter 2.

Let's get into how it all works for each of the major types of content. (And believe me, once you run this process multiple times, it becomes second nature, like you were *born* creating fabulous content.)

Here's how to create content without burnout for...

Your Website and Blog

Your website. Your domain. Your dot com. This is the place where it all happens. This is your brand's "home" on the web. This is where your blog lives, where people can find out about you, and where they will hopefully become customers.

I call this your "content house," and for good reason.

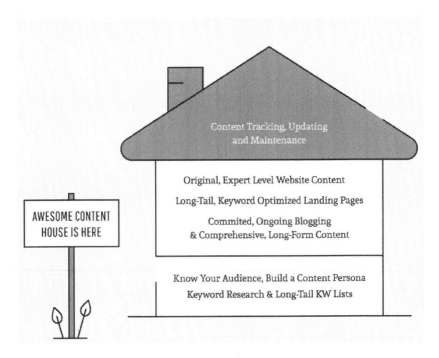

Your house is your personal property. You own the domain, you have the rights to all the content that rests on its foundation. This is in stark contrast to, say, hosting all of your content on a third-party platform like Medium, SquareSpace, Blogger, Weebly, etc. If your entire presence ultimately can be thrown in the trash at the whim of company heads who aren't you, that's a huge problem.

Instead, stake your claim on your own piece of the internet. Pony up the dollars for a domain. You'll have total control over your published content, and it won't vanish someday without your consent or knowledge.

Once your website is up and running, *then* we can talk about content creation. Are you ready? If not, get your domain squared away, first. Then continue.

Here's how to create content without burnout for your blog and website. This includes blog articles and guides as well as foundational website pages like your "about" page, your service pages, and any other landing pages (where people "land" after clicking a link on a call-to-action or an ad).

Stage 1: Website & Blog Content Creation

Remember, the sub-stages for this stage are:

1. Research

2. Ideate

3. Write

4. Edit

Let's get into specifics.

Sub-Stage 1: Research

Research your customers' pain points, questions, and problems. Use what you find to do keyword research, which will form the foundation for the next sub-stage, Ideation.

1. Start with Customer Pain Points

 **Delegate? NO**

How do you create blog and website content that contributes to your business goals?

You start with questions. In particular, you start with questions from *your customers.*

These questions will be the basis for your blog and website content topics. (And when I say "website content," I'm talking about your landing pages, "about" page, product/service pages, and even your homepage.)

Why start with questions?

Because questions = customer pain points.

Think:

What questions are you consistently getting from your prospects?

What questions do they ask over and over again?

What questions are your potential customers searching for on search engines?

These are pain points. They're also your starting points.

As you begin to answer these questions, you'll start to see patterns emerge. You'll see where your visitors are coming from, what they're looking for, and how you can improve their experiences with great blog and website content.

✅ **Pain point examples:**

For Content Hacker, an elite training incubator where we help entrepreneurs get their skills, systems, and strategies down for massive online ROI, some client pain points include:

"how I I verify my course idea before building it"

"how do I grow my business fast"

"where do I find quality writers"

Of course, to get to pain points, I'm assuming you know WHO your customers are. You know their traits, their preferences, their habits, and even their demographics, and have coalesced this vital information into an **audience persona**.

Don't have a clue about any of it? Time to backtrack in your research to square one: investigating your audience.

🔨 **Tools to use at this sub-stage:**

• Audience personas (if you have them)

• Google Analytics – Search under the "Audience" tab

• Facebook Business Insights

• Customer surveys, feedback, & conversations

• Social listening on Twitter, Instagram, Facebook, Reddit, etc.

👉 I've written about audience research (and how to do it) countless times. For laser-focused audience research that cuts way beyond the bland persona, learn more about my Content Transformation© System: contenthacker.com/transformation.

Experts Chime in: Danny Goodwin of Search Engine Journal – *searchenginejournal.com*

> ***Why do we start with the customer in content creation? Because the customer matters most. Ultimately, your content is not about you, but about your customer's problems and concerns.*** Danny Goodwin of Search Engine Journal explains why starting with your audience is nonnegotiable for success:
>
> *Want to increase the number of visitors to your site by 200+%? Content has the power to do that.*
>
> *In June 2017, Search Engine Journal had about 520,000 monthly users. Fast forward to June 2021, and that number grew to just under 1.6 million monthly users.*
>
> *How? What was the secret?*
>
> *Well, it's not really a secret. It's all about creating content for your audience.*
>
> *Creating content that speaks to your target audience or market is the most important thing. Really, it comes down to one simple question: Why should I care? If your content doesn't address this one simple question, from the point of view of your audience, it will fail. Make your audience the center of everything you do.*
>
> *Our mission at Search Engine Journal is to help SEO and digital marketing professionals do their jobs better. We do that by publishing useful, informative, and helpful content.*

If you're creating content just to create content, you're doing it wrong.

If you want to impact lives and grow a large and loyal audience, you do so by answering questions, solving problems, helping them advance their careers, making them more money, or whatever that special thing is that only you can provide.

Everything starts with your audience. But while that is the most important part, it is only the start. Other must-do's:

Optimize your content. Your content must be discoverable via search engines, so make sure you use the keywords and vocabulary of your audience. You want to be sure that whenever people are looking for your content, they can find it.

Promote your content. This can include using social media platforms (Facebook, LinkedIn, Twitter, Instagram, or wherever your audience is), email marketing, and influencers in your space to make sure people know about your content.

Measure the performance of your content. Make sure to figure out what metrics matter to you (is it pageviews, conversions, shares, links, or something else) and measure how your content performed. If you aren't measuring, you're guessing.

Improve and update your content. Your content isn't like a book collecting dust on a shelf. Content is alive. Treat it as such. Improve it & routinely add new information, correct outdated information, and ensure everything is up to date for your audience.

> *My final bit of advice is this: recognize that the content you're creating today may not pay off today or tomorrow. Content is a long game. The content you create today is what will help you in 3 months, 6 months, or maybe even a year from now (this will vary depending on your niche and level of competition).*
>
> *If you're doing all the things right, it will be that much harder to fail. Just don't give up too soon. Success is right around the corner.*

2. Use Pain Points to Research Low-Competition Keywords

 **Delegate? MAYBE** (can D.I.Y. or enlist a content strategist)

Once you have a few client pain points in hand, then you can take them straight to keyword research.

Why keywords? First, they're vital for SEO. If you want to rank at the top of Google, you need to optimize your content for a decent keyword.

I say "decent" because not all keywords are created equal. Not just any word or phrase will be RELEVANT to your business and customers as well as LOW-COMPETITION, which just means it's easy to rank for on Google's first page.

Good news: You already have a trove of keywords waiting for you. Just look to your customer pain points. This is one of the easiest ways to research and find relevant, low-competition key-words: Simply type those pain points into the keyword tool of your choice (I like KWFinder, Semrush, and Ahrefs) and see what comes up.

As I mentioned, at EW, a few customer pain points (framed as keywords) include "how do I start a blog" and "financial blog writing tips." I can take these pain points straight to a keyword tool to find out if they would be worth targeting and writing about in content.

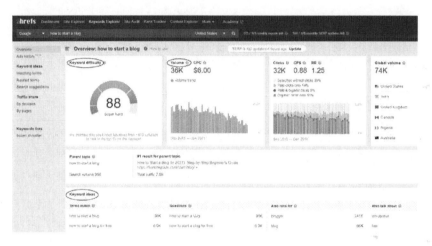

Keyword research often begins with plugging a customer pain point into a keyword research tool. In this example, I'm using Ahrefs.

The main metric to consider when researching keywords/pain points is **keyword difficulty**.

👉 **Keyword difficulty (KD)** – This is an all-in-one metric that tells you how difficult it is to rank for a given keyword. Each tool measures KD slightly differently (though most look at that keyword's results page and check the quality of the websites and pages currently ranking on it).

- KD is measured on a scale of 1 – 100, with a score of 1 meaning the keyword is ridiculously easy to rank for, and 100 meaning the keyword is nearly impossible to rank for.

- **What to look for:** If your site is new, look for keywords with a KD of 40 or below. If your site is established (8 years or more online), you can choose more difficult keywords with a KD of 70 or below.

What about search volume? This is a metric I don't worry about too much—even if it SEEMS low. For example, let's say I find a keyword with a KD of 30 and a search volume of 150. I would still consider this a valuable keyword because: A.) I have a *great* chance of ranking for it on page one with the right content, and B.) Those 150 monthly searchers represent ultra-targeted leads. If they click on my content (and they're extremely likely to if I show up in a high position on page one!), they have a high chance of converting.

It's worth noting that almost all keywords with low search volume will be long-tail and ultra-targeted. The longer and more specific the keyword, the more specific the audience looking for it. This is never a bad thing! Those are the people with the potential to become your customers very quickly, just by checking out your content.

Finally, while you're researching keywords, consider both a focus keyword *and* synonymous keywords for each content piece. Your **focus keyword** is the main keyword you're trying to rank for. It's the *focus* of your content and tied to your overarching topic. It directly informs what information you'll share, and, as a result, you'll use it strategically inside the piece. (This is the keyword you discovered by typing your customer pain points into a keyword research tool.) Meanwhile, **synonymous keywords** are related to the focus keyword and may include synonyms for that word or phrase—alternatives people may use to search for the same topic, just phrased or worded differently. These should be sprinkled here and there throughout your content piece.

☞ Finding synonymous keywords is simple compared to finding focus keywords. Just type your focus keyword into Google, scroll to the bottom of the first page, and check out what's listed under "Related searches".

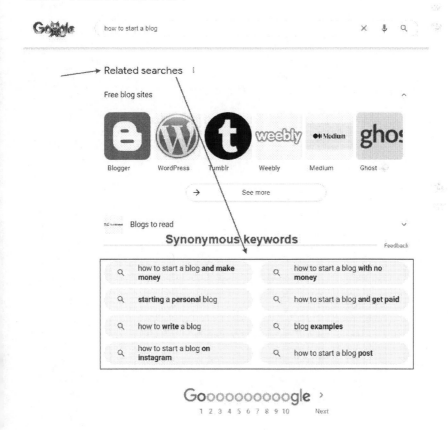

🔨 **Tools to use at this sub-stage:**

- Paid keyword research tools (free tools just don't have the data accuracy you need).

- My favorites: Semrush, Ahrefs, KWFinder

- Google Search (to find related terms/synonymous keywords)

Sub-Stage 2: Ideate

During this stage, you'll take the research you did in Sub-Stage 1 and use it to ideate your website content topics and flesh them out into solid outlines. This is the info you'll hand off to a writer.

1. Brainstorm a Content Topic from Your Focus Keyword

 **Delegate? MAYBE** (can D.I.Y., or enlist a content strategist)

Thanks to the Research sub-stage, you now have a solid keyword in hand that's both relevant to your audience/customers, tied to one of their pain points, and easy to rank for in Google. It's time to take that keyword and start transforming it into content.

Before you can go any further, you need to refine that keyword into a **content topic**. For many keywords, this will be pretty straightforward. For example, if my keyword is "dentist services in Idaho", it's obvious what I'll need to cover in my content piece.

However, if your focus keyword is less straightforward and vaguer, you'll need to do some brainstorming and researching to refine the topic. For instance, a keyword like "ecommerce blog writers" does not immediately mean you should turn it into a content topic. Bottom line, you need more research. Should you create a web page about how to become an ecommerce blog writer? Should your topic involve why this job is important in marketing? Or maybe you should cover how to hire ecommerce blog writers?

Each topic choice is valid, but only one will be what your audience is looking for when they search for "ecommerce blog writers." This is called **search intent**. What is your customer's intent when they type that keyword into the Google search box? You want to get as close to addressing their intent as possible so your content is ultra-relevant to them (which also means Google will rank it highly).

The best way to research search intent and refine your content topic is to use Google itself. Just type in your keyword and do a quick audit of the results that pop up. Which facet of the keyword/topic do they all generally address? To rank, you should go in a similar direction with your topic—but make your content better, more thorough, and more engaging than the current top results. (Easier said than done—more on this later.)

In the screenshot below, you can see the top four results in Google for the keyword "ecommerce blog writers" as well as the "People also ask" Featured Snippet questions. From these results, what do you think the search intent for this keyword is? Which content topic would you write about to rank on this SERP (search engine results page)? *Hint: Most of the results have to do with hiring or finding ecommerce blog writers.*

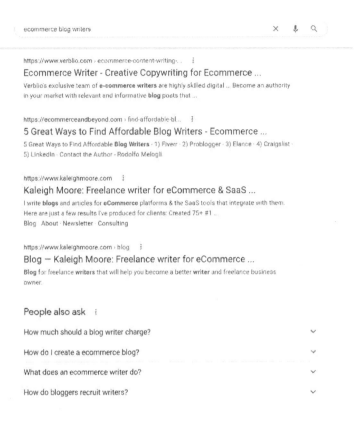

🔨 Tools to use at this sub-stage:

- Google Search

- Most paid keyword research tools also have SERP checkers and SERP analysis features—those can be helpful, too

Experts Chime in: Michael Brenner of Marketing Insider Group – *marketinginsidergroup.com*

If you know your audience well enough, sometimes you can ideate content topics from common problems you see popping up in your industry. These types of topics can be termed "thought leadership" because you're using your expert knowledge to create content that's based on your totally unique perspective. I'm a BIG fan of how *Michael Brenner* does this (and I'll admit, I may or may not do this myself):

For me, writing is therapy. I avoid burnout by seeing the content we produce as helpful. But also cathartic: When something frustrates me, I write about it.

So when I saw marketers wasting money on banner ads, I wrote: "Banners Have 99 Problems and a Click Ain't One." When I saw a client spend five figures on a persona document that provided no actionable direction to their strategy, I wrote: "Personas Are Great Except When They Suck." And when I saw too much boring content coming from B2B brands, I wrote about the need for them to create more snarky, opinionated, and thought leadership content.

Mark Twain said to "Write about what you know." But for me, the best way to avoid burnout is to write about the things that make you mad!

2. Map Your Keyword/Content Topic to a Business Goal

📋 **Delegate? NO**—you need to know your business/sales goals!

Now we're moving steadily along. Here's how far we've come:

We found a *customer pain point* and tied it to...

A low-competition, relevant *focus keyword* that we refined into...

A focused *content topic* connected to our audience's search intent.

From here, we need to keep plotting our map to earning ROI from this content piece. We now need to map our content topic to a **business goal**.

This is where you can make your content work hard for you. Each content piece you publish can and should move you closer to one of your goals. Particularly, think about your sales goals, your brand awareness goals, and your general growth goals (new email subscribers, increase in website traffic, or increase in engagement, for instance). Different kinds of content can help you reach one or many of them. Just consider: What do you want that content piece to DO for your brand?

Connecting Business Goals to Website Content

If you want...

More sales – Add CTAs (calls-to-action) to your content piece that link directly to a sales page, product page, or pages where the customer can book a call with you, try a demo. or otherwise engage your services. We do this at Content Hacker in various places on multiple landing pages, starting with a Learn More that goes straight to a page where we host a free video training where newcomers can learn more about our transformational online business growth program.

Time to build skills and scale your online brand without overload and overwhelm?

You're in the right place. We help creative entrepreneurs Grow a strong digital brand, multiply their revenue, and build long-term skillsets and legacy.

LEARN MORE

WITH JULIA MCCOY

contenthacker.com

More leads – Add CTAs to your content piece that link to a lead magnet, like an ebook, white paper, or some other valuable content that builds further trust with your audience. Here's another example inside. Content Hacker. We give people multiple free download options, so they can choose what they most need:

Write Better Content

Get 15 of the most common writing mistakes that KILL the chances of success for your content before it goes out.

DOWNLOAD NOW

Establish Your Brand

Here's 10 essential truths you need to believe to go from "single creator" to business owner.

DOWNLOAD NOW

Scale Your Brand

Get out of the Chief-Everything-Officer role, escape the burnout, and buckle down on what it takes to scale your brand.

DOWNLOAD NOW

contenthacker.com

More email subscribers – Add CTAs to your content that link directly to a sign-up page or form where your audience can subscribe to your list. Or, add a one-line form so your audience can subscribe, contact you, or request services right inside the content! Content Marketing Institute accomplishes this with a form located in a sidebar next to the main content on their page for consulting services:

news.contentinstitute.com/consulting

Connecting Business Goals to Blog Content

If you want...

More sales – Add CTAs (calls-to-action)) from your blog posts that link directly to your sales page, product page, or page where the customer can book a call with you or try a demo. Here, we're linking directly to an enrollment page for our training program from a Content Hacker blog.

FIND THE RIGHT CONTENT TYPE FOR YOUR UNIQUE BUSINESS GROWTH

If someone asked you "What are some examples of content in your business?", what would you show them?

Is it up to par with the statistics? Meaning, are you truly harnessing the power of this $400 billion industry to your own benefit?

If not, it's time to invest in a mentor who can show you how. I've worked with thousands of clients, learning **what works for a niche and what doesn't**. Working alongside you, I'll show you which type of content will grow YOUR business best, plus the systems and strategies needed to finally break free of the constant hustle and create sustainability and freedom to do what you love.

Ready for monumental change and true sustainability in your business? Learn more about how to build your own long-term small business growth in my Content Transformation System.

The Content Transformation® System:
The last program creative entrepreneurs need to build a self-sufficient business in 90 days.

APPLY TODAY

contenthacker.com/content-types-to-grow-your-business

More leads – Add CTAs to your content piece that link to a lead magnet, like an ebook, white paper, or some other valuable content that builds further trust with your audience. Here's another example inside a Content Hacker blog. The lead magnet is a free, downloadable resource list for marketers-in-training:

contenthacker.com/freelance-writing-jobs

More email subscribers – Add CTAs to your content that link directly to a sign-up page or form where your audience can subscribe. Or, add a one-line form so your audience can subscribe right inside the content! Content Marketing Institute accomplishes this with an email sign-up form located in a sidebar next to the main content (they even sweeten the deal with a free ebook thrown in):

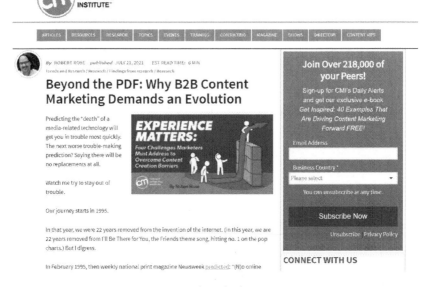

contentmarketinginstitute.com/2021/07/seo-strategy-customer-journey

Whatever the goal(s) you choose, ensure each content piece has one, even if it's as simple as growing brand awareness and building that coveted trust with readers (which requires zero CTAs, though I always recommend including at least one at the end of your post—it tells your reader exactly what to do when they're done reading and where they can place their growing trust, and if your content is good enough, they'll follow through).

Your content can absolutely help you advance toward your goals. You just need to give it a chance... and a few well-placed CTAs.

🔨 Tools to use at this sub-stage:

- Your business goals + content goals, which should be documented in a content strategy.

- No content strategy? Learn how to build one at
contentstrategycourse.com

3. Determine the Word Count for Your Content Piece

 **Delegate? NO**

Word count matters in content. The right amount of words in a piece will give readers satisfaction when they're done reading. They'll have found the answers they needed, plus ones they didn't *know* they needed.

If your content is unsatisfactory (and you can tell this by lack of traction, conversions, or by the bounce rate—the percentage of people who click away soon after landing on your site, or who leave your site without further exploration), you probably need more words, and better ones, to explain whatever you're talking about in a web page or blog.

To determine the right word count for any content piece on any topic, look at the top three results in Google for your keyword. What is the average word count among them? Ideally, you need to produce better content than what is contained within those results. Often, but not always, better content = more words.

The word count I rely on to "beat the top three" is 2,000 words. This is the standard I give my content writers. They know this is usually what they're aiming for when they write my content. However, if they find the topic requires more words as they write—and, by the way, experienced writers have an instinct for this—they know they can simply write more and I'll pay more.

Keep in mind: holding a standard doesn't always play out in real life. I never rely on it blindly; I always check Google first. Good example: The SERP for the keyword "how to start a blog" has four results with *well over 6,000 words*. One of them tops 10k!! (Ryan Robinson authored that one—I know him personally, and he only writes epic content. *insert clapping sound*)

If I wanted to try to rank for "how to start a blog", my 2,000-word standard would be measly and inadequate, here. That's why you should never rely on a set number for word count for every single piece. Some content requires MORE words, and some content requires LESS words to thoroughly explore the topic in a way that satisfies readers. Thus, always check the results page for your keyword and see what **the top three results** are demanding (if you want to beat them, that is). There's no need to look beyond to the top five or top 10. Then, give that word count to your writer. In the instance above, I would average out the word count of the top three results of Google and shoot for that. That means I'd tell my writer to aim for 6,800-7,000 words.

🔨 **Tools to use at this sub-stage:**

- Google Search

- Your human eye

4. Produce a Fully-Formed Topic and Outline (and Write It Down!)

 Delegate? NO

At this point, you should have your focus keyword, topic, and desired word count in hand for your new piece of web page content. Now it's time to create an outline, one your writer will follow to structure and write your web page.

A lot of people side-eye the outlining process. You may see it as an unnecessary step, but I'm here to tell you it is absolutely, 100%, without a doubt, totally and utterly *necessary.* Here's why: Your outline is your roadmap to how you want the finished content piece to look, feel, and read. The outline helps you ensure you include all the important points, their order, and any other key information, like keywords.

Structure is SO important to creating great content. It influences readability perhaps just as much as the writing quality itself.

It helps your content attract AND retain your readers' attention. And it's gigantic for SEO, as search engines use headings as a guide as they crawl content, noting importance (which keywords are in the H1? The H2s?), relationships (how do the nested H3s relate to the H2?), and order.

How do you build a solid, strong structure for each piece of content in your pipeline? It all starts with your outline. This is the framework of your content, and you cannot ignore it.

Remember those tedious, painful outlines you had to write for Composition 101 in college or English classes in high school? Forget them. Outlining doesn't have to be so meticulous and strict (unless, of course, that's how you prefer to do it—no judgments here). For me, I prefer loose outlines that guide my writers toward a structure, rather than determining that structure myself. I may mention points I want covered and resources to use, but I leave the building to my writer—that's part of their job, and a good writer will have major skills for structuring content for search engines and readers.

Here's what I include, in a bullet-pointed list for reference:

- **Desired word count** (I stipulate this as a general number to aim for—as my writers write, they will get a better feel for whether the topic will need more or fewer words to be satisfying to read, and will let me know. I adjust pay as needed.)

- **Focus keyword**

- **Synonymous keywords** to sprinkle in (pulled from Google, see point #2 in this section)

- **Headline** (sometimes I create one, sometimes I leave it to my writer)

- **Resources/points to include** (links with studies/data I particularly want to be mentioned, facets of the topic I want to home in on, etc.)

- Optional: **Points to research** (e.g. "Research top marketing jobs and their salaries")

- Optional: **Formatting/structuring notes** (e.g. "include a list [H2] with numbered points underneath [each an H3]")

- Optional: **Top content ranking in Google to outdo**

- Optional: **Inspirational pieces** (links to articles you love/want to emulate)

Here's an example of an actual outline I gave to one of my writers for a blog that performed exceptionally well (see it live at *contenthacker.com/women-in-marketing*). It's important to note that this went to a writer that has been writing and researching marketing topics for **five years** (aka, they are a specialist and know what they're doing on this topic).

Content Format: Long-Form SEO Blog

Writer Outline for 1 Content Hacker Blog

Persona: Advanced executives *Real client example*

Voice/Style: Zero fluff. Actionable. Fun, engaging, yet not too "funsies" or light. Deep. Far beyond superficial.

3000w-4000w

Topic: 50 Women in Marketing To Follow

Keyword: women in marketing

women in marketing

📍 Anywhere 🌐 Any Language

32 / 100
POSSIBLE
Keyword Difficulty

640
Search Volume

Monthly Searches | Trends

Follow a standardized format, 70w per featured person – this will equal a 3500w blog. Make sure to include a site if they have a site/personal brand and include their Twitter handles. Please do proper in-depth research to make sure this is a diverse list. Include women that may not get featured often but deserve to be.

Articles to study and outperform:

https://www.toprankblog.com/2018/11/25-women-digital-marketing-2018/

https://www.digitalmarketer.com/blog/women-in-marketing/

https://womeninmarketing.org.uk/

https://www.worldforumdisrupt.com/women-in-market-ing-la-2020/

https://www.searchenginejournal.com/female-marketers/296785/

https://co.agencyspotter.com/top-20-women-marketing/

https://www.monster.com/career-advice/article/women-in-marketing

Download the full template: contenthacker.com/free-outline

Now, while this is specifically a blog outline, it doesn't differ much from the web page outlines I also create for my writers. Web pages have different purposes from blogs in terms of the goals you're trying to hit, but the general structure is often very similar.

Last but not least: Write down your topic and focus keyword in a content calendar to keep track of it! I keep my content ideas in a tab on my calendar called "Ideation." Once I write an outline and send it off to a writer for creation, I remove the topic from "Ideation", add it to my main calendar, and schedule it so I know that idea is off the table.

🔨 **Tools to use at this sub-stage:**

- See tools from Ideation sub-stages #1-3

5. Schedule Your Content Piece, Assign to a Writer, & Track It

📝 **Delegate? MAYBE (you *could*, if you have a writer you trust that is expert at handling your niche/topics —otherwise, D.I.Y.)**

Here's where your content calendar becomes a champion in your content operation. It gives you a bird's eye view of which content pieces are in production, which are ready to schedule, and which are scheduled.

Now, for web page content, scheduling is a bit different than it is for blog content. Pages are foundational pieces, while blogs are more ephemeral. You should be constantly publishing new blogs, but only publishing web content as needed, or to take advantage of SEO opportunities. For the most part, web pages remain static for long periods. They also contain vital information about your business, your services, and you. Think of it this way: Blogs are dynamic. Web pages are static. Blogs are ever-changing, with new posts going out regularly. Web pages don't change often.

When you create new web pages or update old ones, you can absolutely schedule it on your content calendar just as you would with blogs. The difference is, blog scheduling must be a lot more strategic regarding *when* it goes live, because your blog feed is just one more channel flowing into the river of dynamic internet content. (Other channels: Twitter/Instagram/Facebook feeds. YouTube channels. News updates. And thousands of other blog feeds from creators like you.) To maximize visibility, blogs need to be published when the greatest amount of people are paying attention. Web pages? Not so much. Nobody is following your website for new page updates. (They ARE following your blog for new posts.)

In general, scheduling content means assigning it a specific day and time when it will go live on your website. Once the piece is published, the assigned date becomes the "published" date. This means, along with knowing exactly what the future holds for your content, you also know precisely what has been published and when. This is incredibly important to keep track of, not just because it will prevent you from creating duplicate content (which is an SEO no-no), but also because your content record will help you ideate future content topics.

Imagine: You're doing topic research for a new web page on your site. You want to create an in-depth page on a service you offer—what it's about, who needs it, how it works, etc. You check your calendar for what you've published on the topic. You see that you've already created an informational page about the service targeting a broader keyword. You decide to create additional pages that support that page, each covering a different facet of the service in more depth, each targeting a long-tail keyword related to the initial broad term. With this strategy, you can link to your broader page from the supporting pages—a great move for SEO.

Finally, your content calendar can also help you keep track of which writer is responsible for which content piece. Once you assign your writer a topic and send them an outline, just add their name to the record for that content.

Past + present + future, all in one simple tool, all at your disposal to leverage as needed. That's the beauty of scheduling and the wisdom of the content calendar.

🔨 Tools to use at this sub-stage:

- Content calendar tool (Airtable, Trello, Notion, even a Google spreadsheet works)

Sub-Stage 3: Write

You'll be largely absent from this sub-stage because your writer will handle pulling together the content piece from the topic, outline, and word count you formulated during Ideation. That said, it's still essential to understand the ins and outs of this incredibly important step in the process, so listen up. (Your writer is toiling hard!)

📝 **Delegate? YES**—hire an expert writer (and an editor/QA if you think you need one)!

So, you've handed off the outline to your content writer. While you wait for the finished product, there are some important points to remember about this step of the process.

If you're not a writer by trade, this sub-stage may seem mysterious to you. You send off a skeleton of an idea, and in the end, your writer (ideally) sends back a fully rounded, polished piece that reads like a dream. How in the heck does B flow from A? Here's a rundown of the steps your writer may be following as they create your content. While not every writer has the same method, most will follow something closely resembling this trail of creation.

1. Draft a Headline

Unless you provided a headline to use, your writer will probably draft various versions of one until they hit the right combination of words. They may draft as few as two or three versions, or as many as 20 (!). They'll structure it in different ways, play with the verbs and adjectives, and, if they're smart, insert it in a couple of headline checkers to see how it scores for readability, engagement, and SEO.

2. Review Inspiration

Remember those inspirational articles you included in your outline? Your writer will peruse them and note the structure, the information included, and how keywords are used inside them.

3. Draft a Compelling Introduction

Your writer will spend extra time perfecting this part of your content, especially the hook that draws in the reader. Ultimately, the intro sets up the reader so they know: A.) Exactly what they're in for if they keep reading, i.e., the answer to "Why should I care?" and B.) The answer to the question they were asking Google, or the direct response that resolves their search intent.

4. Draft H2s and H3s

Following the outline you provided, your writer will draft the main subheaders of the content. Here they'll decide what points to cover, insert important keywords naturally and strategically, decide how to structure points and in what order, and how to word subheaders in unique, powerful, and compelling ways.

5. Find External and Internal Links

Once they get into the meat of writing your content, your scribe will start looking for leading statistics and facts (external links/ citations) that will support the points they want to make. (If you provided some, your writer will weave them in.) They'll also look for opportunities to link to relevant content from your site (internal links). This means your writer will link to a related blog or web page on your site that will further clarify the topic. Both of these practices are great for SEO.

5. Draft the Body and Refine

As they write, your writer will continually go back over their work and check that all the points flow, cut any fluff that creeps in, and look for opportunities to add more research and data for impact. They'll also source images and screenshots, if relevant.

6. Draft a Conclusion

The concluding H2 is an important place to wrap up the content, add necessary CTAs, and close in a satisfying way for the reader. Your writer will give extra attention to crafting this part of the content.

7. Self-Edit and Refine Further

Once the writer adds the last period to the conclusion, the work isn't over. From this point, they'll work backward and re-check the overall flow and structure of the piece. Is the most important point at the top? Do the other points flow logically and satisfyingly? They may also further tweak the headline and introduction. Then they'll edit the entire piece, reading from the beginning as if they're the target audience. Your writer will self-edit for spelling, factual inaccuracies, word choice and tone, grammar, and keyword usage. At this point, they may use a spelling or grammar checker as an extra set of "eyes."

8. Let the Piece "Rest"

At this point, your writer will probably step away from the content for a while so they can return later with fresh eyes. When you're in a muddle of writing, it's easy to get too close to a piece and become "blind" to even the simplest of errors. Stepping away usually solves this problem.

9. Finalize and Send!

After a final read-through and round of edits, your writer will save the piece and send it off for your approval.

Tools to use at this sub-stage:

- Word processor (Microsoft Word, Google Docs)

- Headline checker (AMI Headline Analyzer, CoSchedule's Headline Analyzer/Headline Studio)

- An advanced spelling/grammar/readability checker (Grammarly, Hemingway App, Readable)

- An online thesaurus

- The outline/content brief you created in Ideation

- Google Search

Experts Chime in: Brian Dean of Backlinko – *backlinko.com*

It's easy to get burned out as a creator, whether you're ideating, researching, strategizing, or doing the actual writing/creating. Brian Dean has some inspiration on how to push through it:

The #1 thing that's helped me avoid burnout is committing to a small amount of writing every day (approximately 500-1,000 words).

The writing can be for my blog, YouTube video scripts, courses, and more. The key is to do a little bit each day no matter what. And to leave "a little in the tank" for the next day.

I usually get burned out when I take too much on at one time. And this slow-and-steady approach helps me keep things moving without feeling overwhelmed.

Experts Chime in: Masooma Memon, Freelance Writer for B2B SaaS and eCommerce, *inkandcopy.com*

Masooma Memon is a freelance writer who counts companies like DataBox, Vimeo, ConvertFlow, and more among her clients. She shares no-nonsense writing advice and more on Twitter @ inkandcopy, where she has a devoted following. Whether you're ideating and strategizing hard or taking on some content writing yourself, check out Masooma's great tips for keeping burnout at bay:

1. Take "no-writing, no-content-creation" days weekly.

Ideally, every Sunday forget that you have to create content and unwind. Don't think about new content ideas or promotion tactics. Instead, try to unplug completely—no emails, no social.

Doing so gives your brain the break it deserves, refreshing and recharging it to the point that you'll enjoy content production the next week all while keeping burnout at bay.

A similar approach is to take a long weekend or a few days off to disconnect and do something that'll charge you. I disconnected for a week to read my favourite novel series—it fixed my burnout significantly.

P.S. Yes, regular breaks during the day work, but a no-content-creation day or week helps me tremendously in keeping burnout away.

2. Regularly shake up your content creation processes and routine.

This breaks the monotony of your work — something that can easily push you to burnout.

Every once in a while as I find myself getting bored of the "same old," I switch my routine ever so slightly.

Massive shifts in your workflow and style can impact productivity. So I prefer to make small changes.

Examples:

I'll work in the outline document itself instead of a new draft document, elaborating points I've written under each header.

I'll think on the page so much so that the first draft is almost ready to go. Ideally, I prefer writing a rough first draft, then rewriting as needed.

3. Free writing.

Content creation comes with a lot of mental workload. To someone else, you're sitting at your desk, tapping away at your keyboard. In reality though, all the thinking that goes into writing is mentally exhausting you.

A good solution to get yourself to produce content even if you're tired (but tied by deadlines and commitments): free writing. Type without thinking much. You'll soon get into a flow state where you'll churn out not just average content, but good content for your first draft (this works best if you've thoroughly researched the topic beforehand/know the subject well and have an outline ready).

Sub-Stage 4: Edit (A.K.A. Approval)

During this stage, you'll review the completed content piece after the writer writes and self-edits it (or, depending on your process, after a QA edits it). You'll either approve it wholesale or, if it's not quite there, send it back for revisions. This is also the stage where you will personalize the piece if needed, if publishing under your name.

Delegate? NO—the last word on your content pieces should be yours.

When you reach sub-stage 4, your writer will have already edited their work at least a few times. (As you've learned, self-editing is a major part of the writing process.) Now you're receiving that work into your hands. When it lands on your desk, what do you do with it? Should you send it straight to publishing? Should you edit it with a fine-tooth comb? Should you check for errors and send it back to your writer every time you find a new one, even if it's just a missing word or a misplaced comma?

No. No. No, and no. The writer you hire should be sending you highly-polished work, and if they're *not*, you might need to have a discussion with them or find a better writer. If you choose to hire an editor to check all the content coming through your writing team, the need for major editing on your end drops even more substantially. By the time each piece reaches your desk, your job is more about *reviewing* rather than editing, and more about ensuring overarching checkpoints are hit rather than poring over minute details.

For example, when a new web content piece hits your inbox, sent fresh from the writer, grammar and spelling shouldn't be issues. Instead, you should be looking at the bigger picture.

Does the piece work as a whole?

Is it thorough enough? Is it satisfying to read?

Does it hit the mark for the topic and focus keyword?

Are there opportunities for it to be more personal? Could you add personal stories or details your writer wouldn't know, but would enrich the piece?

That's it. Usually, most pieces should need only a cursory glance and a quick scan to ensure all of the above questions are answered. A lot of pieces won't need personal touches from you—so as long as you think to yourself, "Yes!" as you're reading the content, "editing" in the traditional sense of the word is unnecessary.

The above scenario is common after you've established a long-running working relationship with a writer. What if you've just hired a writer, and they're still learning your expectations, how you want your content written, and your brand's voice/tone?

You're probably going to get a few pieces that miss the mark at first. But this is NOT a reason to fire them from your team in favor of hiring someone else who will "get it" immediately. Newsflash: That's never going to happen. Every writer you hire needs a grace period and training to get in the groove, understand what you want, and deliver it. To see long-term success with them, you need to have patience and stay the course. Because the writer you train and mentor will become the writer you can count on to produce great content with little oversight from you in the future. Hand them an outline, and they'll come back with *exactly* what you're looking for, *but only if you do the work and invest in their talent and skill.*

This means, as you settle in with a new writer, you'll have to do more editing and revising in the traditional sense. You'll have to take time to give them feedback and notes, and give them a chance to learn what they need to know to write for you successfully. In this scenario, give them grace. Note where they're missing the mark, but also note where they're nailing it. Send back the piece for revisions. A good writer will eventually learn what you want and need from your content, so you'll barely have to edit their work in the future.

Bottom line: Investing in a talented writer NOW will result in a major return on investment for your entire content operation and content marketing strategy. It will also equal mega time savings during the edit/approval sub-stage.

🔨 **Tools to use at this sub-stage:**

- Your intimate knowledge of your brand, customers, and content goals

Sub-Stage 5: Images

The final Creation sub-stage is all about the finishing touches that will set your content apart from the rest of the heap.

📝 **Delegate? YES**—enlist a graphic designer to make your image assets shine.

Finally, one of the most important pieces of creating written content is adding images. Images have a major impact on engagement—one study found that the mere presence of an image in a post was enough to boost it significantly.[1]

For blogs, a best practice is to include screenshots interspersed with the content (or possibly memes or GIFs, depending on your brand voice). For website content, you may have image assets to include that complement the overarching design of your site, or special image/design elements that set off various pieces of information. For both website *and* blog content, however, custom images are a must. This means branded header images and CTAs at a minimum.

What do I mean by "custom"? Specifically, images created for your brand that include your logo and brand colors. They should be sized correctly for both displaying crisp and clear on the page, and for appearing in social media feeds. Need examples? Check out this blog from Easelly. At the top of the page, alongside the headline, you'll find a custom-designed header image that fits the blog topic and ties into Easelly's branding.

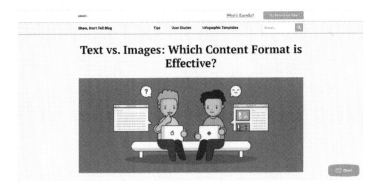

easel.ly/blog/text-vs-images-which-content-format-effective

Sure, you could cheap out and instead just grab a free, unedited stock image from a random site, but I'm here to tell you that this makes your brand look cheap, too. Every time I see a bland stock image at the top of another blog, I want to click away, because usually the accompanying content will be bland and useless, too. On the other hand, I've noticed if a company invests in their branding and images, they're more likely to invest in the quality of their content. **That's a trust differentiator, for sure.**

Why *wouldn't* you want to differentiate from the thousands of brands who didn't bother to put care and investment into their *entire* presence, from the text and content to the images and assets? Why *wouldn't* you want to look like you have your sh!t together from the first moment a potential customer discovers your brand?

To drive the point home, let's look at another blog on a similar topic to the one above. However, this blog includes an unedited, as-is stock image at the top.

EMAIL MARKETING | SALES EMAILS

Images vs. No Images in Email Marketing Newsletters: Which Gets Better Results?

NEXT ARTICLE

Let's just call this one computer.jpg

Which blog stands out more? Which blog can you instantly associate with a brand? Most importantly... which blog would you rather read? The one with the bland image of a computer, which you've probably seen one million times in various iterations, or the blog with the unique custom image that tells a story?

I know which one I'm reading.

🔨 Tools to use at this sub-stage:

- Your graphic designer! Backtrack to Chapter 2 for hiring tips.

Stage 2: Website & Blog Content Publishing

The sub-stages for Stage 2, Publishing, include:

- Schedule & Draft

- Post

Let's break it down.

Sub-Stage 1: Schedule & Draft

This stage is when your piece transforms from a document or file to a living, breathing content piece that resides in your content management system (CMS), like WordPress. This stage takes it from doc to living draft.

📝 **Delegate? YES**—hire a blog editor to draft pieces to WordPress and publish them on dates you specify in your content calendar.

Your finished content piece is ready for publishing. But wait! Don't copy-paste into WordPress and click "Publish" quite yet.

There's some important work to do before your content is ready to go live.

1. Optimize

Your content will gain more traction in Google—and with readers—if you optimize it, first. After all, you spent the time and effort to find a focus keyword and synonymous terms to include in your content. It would be an absolute waste not to take it all the way to "optimized" with some key techniques using WordPress and Yoast SEO (an all-star WordPress plugin that helps you fully optimize your content once it hits your CMS).

For my blogs and content, I adhere to a checklist for optimization *every single time* a webpage or blog post is set to go live. Each step stays the same whether I'm the one drafting in WordPress, or my blog editor is doing it.

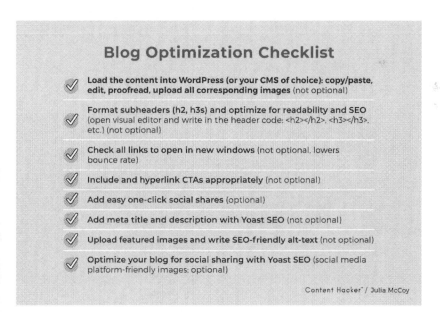

Blog Optimization Checklist

- ✅ **Load the content into WordPress (or your CMS of choice): copy/paste, edit, proofread, upload all corresponding images** (not optional)
- ✅ **Format subheaders (h2, h3s) and optimize for readability and SEO** (open visual editor and write in the header code: <h2></h2>, <h3></h3>, etc.) (not optional)
- ✅ **Check all links to open in new windows** (not optional, lowers bounce rate)
- ✅ **Include and hyperlink CTAs appropriately** (not optional)
- ✅ **Add easy one-click social shares** (optional)
- ✅ **Add meta title and description with Yoast SEO** (not optional)
- ✅ **Upload featured images and write SEO-friendly alt-text** (not optional)
- ✅ **Optimize your blog for social sharing with Yoast SEO** (social media platform-friendly images; optional)

Content Hacker™ / Julia McCoy

2. Schedule

Once the content is loaded into WordPress and optimized, think about when you'll post it. Do you have a set schedule for posting blogs you need to follow (e.g., you post one blog every Wednesday morning at 8 a.m.)? Or does the content tie into a specific date, event, or launch? If the latter is true, schedule strategically so the content will go live on that date (or near it).

🔨 Tools to use at this sub-stage:

- Yoast SEO for WordPress

- Content calendar

- Your trusty blog editor

Sub-Stage 2: Post

Ready to go from draft to live? This simple stage includes the physical process of posting your content so the world can see it.

📝 **Delegate? YES**—your blog editor can post your content for you, following your schedule outlined in your content calendar.

This sub-stage is as simple as simple gets. Everything else should be finished up to this point: content ideating, researching, writing, editing, drafting, and optimizing. The complete piece should be ready to go and waiting for you to post in your CMS. Except, I recommend freeing up your time and leaving the physical part of publishing—clicking the "Publish" button—to your blog editor.

What about scheduling posts to auto-publish at a time/date you specify? Personally, I don't rely on this feature. Quite often, posts

I pre-scheduled in WordPress failed to publish at the specified time, which created a ripple effect of broken links and missing content in the promotional email I sent out for said content. Instead of relying on unreliable WordPress for this, I ask my blog editor to physically hit "Publish" at the date/time specified in the content calendar. That way, I always know the blog is live at the right time.

🔨 Tools to use at this sub-stage:

- Content calendar

- Your content management system (CMS), like WordPress

- Your trusty blog editor

Stage 3: Website & Blog Content Promotion

You made it to the final stage of website and blog content creation! *throws confetti* And, by the way, this is one stage many people on a time or budget crunch skip, but you do NOT want to do that. Often, it's during the promotion stage that your content really takes off. This is because you're not relying on chance or fate to ensure people see it—you're physically pushing it out into the world so as many eyes as possible will land on it. (And after *that*, SEO will do quite a bit to ensure your target readers keep discovering it months, potentially years, later.)

But first, to give it its best chance, you need to promote it when it's hot and fresh.

Remember, the two sub-stages that fall under Promotion are:

- Email

- Social media

Here's what to do next.

 Experts Chime in: Adrienne Barnes of Best Buyer Personas – *bestbuyerpersona.com, adriennenakohl.com*

While blog content is a fantastic foundation for any business, it's not the only option. Adrienne Barnes, a B2B SaaS content marketer who has worked with companies like Drift, ActiveCampaign, Foundr, and more, describes how she found the sweet spot with content for her busy lifestyle, one that still helped grow her business:

As a solo founder, homeschooling momma, and consultant to B2B SaaS companies, I've had to learn to create content and grow my business in ways that work best for my schedule, my family's needs, and my strengths. For me, this meant not attempting to keep up with everyone else. I struggled writing LinkedIn posts every day but found myself easily sharing ideas, tactics, and learnings on Twitter.

As a previous content writer, I thought I would be able to easily crank out blog posts on topics specific to my offerings, but that wasn't the case, I struggled to find large chunks of time required to get into the flow of writing, but I could easily record an hour-long workshop or podcast with detailed information.

> *As soon as I began to notice and appreciate all the content I was creating (I had this assumption that blog posts and ebooks were all that mattered) I was able to lean into those formats and plat-forms more. Because I am my business, it's vital that I enjoy the work I'm doing and work in a way that is natural to me, not just an algorithm or current trend.*

Sub-Stage 1: Email

Time to tell your email subscribers about your freshly published content. Luckily, email promotion doesn't have to be difficult. In fact, it has the potential to be one of the simplest steps you'll complete.

This sub-stage is an incredibly simple yet vital part of the content promotion process. According to Campaign Monitor's industry benchmarks report, the average open rate for emails stands at a whopping 18%.[4] Email matters, people! (More on this in the next section, *Your Email List.*)

Want to see just how simple email promotion is? There are only two steps:

1. Write a short email promoting your blog. Add a CTA at the end pointing to said blog.

2. Schedule it to send to your list when the blog goes live.

Let's break each one down further.

1. Write a Short Email Promoting Your Blog

Delegate? MAYBE—you can create very simple promotional emails yourself, or you can assign the task to your social media manager or even your writer. (For creation steps, jump to the next section: **Your Email List.**)

Blog promotion emails don't have to be fancy. You don't have to write award-winning copy or reinvent the wheel to get the job done.

After all, your task here is clear. You need to alert your email subscribers that you've just published new content. On some level, they have an interest in reading it. (After all, they subscribed, didn't they?) All you need to do is add in a little extra persuasion, because, well, inboxes can be unwieldy things. Many of your subscribers will be battling mountains of promotional emails from all kinds of companies—sale alert emails from their favorite consumer goods and clothing brands, newsletters from small businesses or influencers they support, new product launch emails, email sequences they got sucked into, emails from their subscriptions services, and more. Somehow, you need to elbow your way in there so they actually SEE your message, period.

In short, blog promotions emails don't need to be fancy. They DO need to be persuasive to some degree, without feeling like you're desperate or slimy. You also don't want to spend hours agonizing over your email copy. And, if you're on a budget, you don't want to break the bank, either.

My solution? Tap into the expert copy you already had written for you during the Creation stage. My favorite strategy is to take the introduction from the blog, add a few transition sentences at the end to segue to your CTA, and...

Et voila! Done. Here's an example straight from my playbook (this also appears back in Chapter 2):

2. Schedule & Send to Your List

🗒️ Delegate? MAYBE

Once your promo email is ready, you can schedule it to go out to your list via your email marketing tool. (I personally use ConvertKit.) This is such a super-easy step, I usually do it myself. However, your blog editor or your social media manager can be trained to do it, too. Always schedule your promo email to go out to your subscribers *after* the blog goes live, on the day of publishing.

🔨 Tools to use at this sub-stage:

- Email marketing tool (ConvertKit, Mailchimp, AWeber, GetResponse, Lead Pages—there are a TON to choose from, and many are free)

👉 For more in-depth guidance on email content creation, head to **Your Email List.**

Sub-Stage 2: Social Media

Social media promotion is just as vital as email. If you want more eyes on your content, you need to tell people it exists. This stage is about writing short, promotional posts for your chosen platforms. You'll also need share-worthy images, which you should have at the ready from completing the Creation stage.

Everything is happening on social media these days. But you don't need me to tell you that. You're probably right there, opening up Instagram or Twitter or Facebook whenever you have a spare minute. That's partly why promoting your blog to your favorite platforms is so important: Most of us are connected through social media in some way—72.3% of Americans actively use social media sites every month.[5] That includes your prospects, followers, customers, and fans.

Plus, 94% of bloggers say they use social media to drive traffic to their content.[6] That's because it works. *That* means you need to get on your socials and spread the word about your new blogs and articles. They need every little boost you can give!

There are three steps to social media promotion for your content:

3. Promote New Blog Posts and Content

4. Develop a Presence on the Most Relevant Platforms for Your Brand

5. Engage With Your Audience

Let's go.

1. Promote New Blog Posts and Content (with a Social Media Scheduling App)

✎ **Delegate? YES**—hand off to your social media manager UNLESS the posts are coming from your personal profile (see *Chapter 2: DO or DON'T Delegate These Tasks*)

Promoting new content on social media means writing posts and/or captions for each platform on which your brand maintains a presence. If this makes you shudder, I get you. Each platform, whether you're tweeting on Twitter, creating posts and reels on Instagram, or just updating your Facebook business page, has its own set of rules and best practices for posting so you get the most traction possible. Unless you're an expert whose job entails knowing all the ins and outs, it might be too much to keep up with.

For that reason, outsource this piece of content promotion to your social media manager. The right person will have their fingers on the pulse of what works for the major channels and what doesn't. They'll have the skill to write engaging posts that promote your new blog or content piece in a non-slimy way.

👉 Need help hiring the right person? Head back to Chapter 2, to the section **How to Find the RIGHT Partners & Make Delegation 1000% Easier.**

Before handing off writing social media posts and scheduling them, make sure you have your social media scheduling app set up. I love MeetEdgar because of the smart post recycling feature, and the customizable schedule features you can set up for each post. Set up profiles and schedules first, then give your social media manager the reins to manage the app.

2. Develop a Presence on the Most Relevant Platforms for Your Brand

📝 **Delegate? YES**—hand off to your social media manager UNLESS the posts are coming from your personal profile

Developing a brand presence on social media is necessary for a myriad of reasons, but the most obvious is that, without an audience who will actually *see* your content promotion posts, your efforts will fall into the void. And no one likes wasted effort.

How do you develop a presence on your chosen social platforms? For one, post regularly. Develop a schedule for posting and stick to it. Your social media manager can help you out with this. Beyond blog promo posts, what else will your audience engage with? This might depend on your industry and niche, so it's important to get a feel for industry standards as well as creative ways to differentiate your posts. The biggest factor to focus on first, though, is posting regularly and providing value through your posts—just like with written content.

3. Engage With Your Audience

🗒 **Delegate? YES**—hand off to your social media manager UNLESS the posts are coming from your personal profile

The final step of social media promotion: Engage with your audience. And "engaging" might look different on different platforms. On Instagram, it's replying to comments, having conversations in your DMs (whether they spring from a Story, a Reel, or evolve from engaging with a person regularly), sharing others' posts and Stories, and just being active and present.

For branded accounts, a great way to engage with your audience is to simply stay responsive. Genuinely reply to comments and answer questions. If someone has an issue they take to your brand account, try to resolve it with diplomacy and kindness. Your social media manager can really help you out, here. As your brand grows, it might get harder and harder to engage authentically due to the sheer volume of comments, DMs, notifications, mentions, and other bells and whistles pulling at your attention. Your social media manager can step in, sift through it all, and help engage where needed.

Ultimately, engagement helps promotion because it builds a re-lationship with your audience. When your content promo posts come out, they'll be more likely to click or check out your link if they feel connected to you. And, by the way, they *won't* feel con-nected if you try to manufacture engagement inauthentically, or fail to engage—read: canned responses, no response at all to people who reach out first, slow response times, repeatedly dis-appearing for weeks only to reappear out of the blue, buying likes and followers, etc.

When it comes down to it, use your common sense. Be a human person. How would you like the brands you follow to respond to you, engage with you? Do that.

🔨 Tools to use at this sub-stage:

- Your social media scheduling app of choice (MeetEdgar, AgoraPulse, Buffer, Sprout Social, CoSchedule—there are reams of options)

- Your deep knowledge of your audience and where they tend to hang out on social

The Content Hacker™ Process Map

Your A-Z Downloadable, Streamlined Visual Process for Building and Publishing Content

"I run a content marketing agency and we are at the scaling stage, and the Process Map is just what I needed, especially your Airtable templates." — Jessica Bennett, Owner and Content Creator at Got Writer's Block

Get the Process Map today: contenthacker.com/processmap

Your Email List

The humble email list is perhaps one of the best tools at your disposal for content promotion. With this simple technology that's been around for about 56 years[2] (!!), you have the power to directly reach people who have given their permission for one-to-one contact with you.

That fact right there, that people will allow your emails to take up space in their personal inboxes, where messages and notifications from their friends and family also reside, is a giant indicator of trust built. If you have subscribers, you have another level of audience: people who don't just read your content or interact with your brand, but think you're worth hearing from at times they *don't solicit*. Your email can show up in their inbox whenever, and they may have an interest in reading it. That's powerful, and that's why your email list should be treated with the utmost **respect**.

As we've discussed, building trust with your prospects and customers is more important than ever. For one, ever since the pandemic began in early 2020, consumer trust in information sources has dropped to an all-time low.[3]

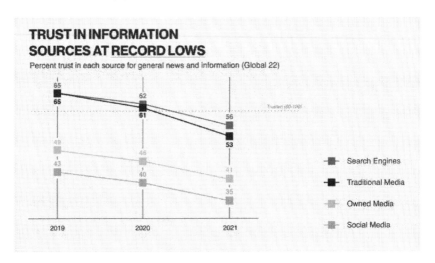

edelman.com/trust/2021-trust-barometer

The key here, however, is to remember when consumers lost faith in traditional media and other sources, they turned to businesses instead.[3]

So, gaining that coveted trust means you must not toss it out the window by sending your subscribers throwaway emails with no value or spamming them with annoying offers three times a day. Think about them as people, and consider them in terms of maintaining a relationship.

As you build up a great email content marketing process, consider these stages and sub-stages:

Stage 1: Email Content Creation

> » Sub-Stage 1: Audience/Segmentation
>
> » Sub-Stage 2: Goals
>
> » Sub-Stage 3: Write

- ## Stage 2: Email Content Publishing

> » Sub-Stage 1: Scheduling and Frequency
>
> » Sub-Stage 2: Sending to Your List

For nitty-gritty details, let's dive into Stage 1: Email Content Creation.

Stage 1: Email Content Creation

Sub-Stage 1: Audience/Segmentation

As with any other type of content creation, creating great emails means starting with your audience and understanding their needs and interests.

 **Delegate? NO**—know your audience!

Before you ever think about creating a single email, you must first think about WHO you're writing to and how you can segment that audience into groups you can target with more personalized, relevant messages. This is called **segmentation**, and it's the future of successful email content.

82% of marketers say they see increased open rates thanks to email segmentation/personalization. Another 75% say they see higher email click-through rates, and 58% say they see increased customer satisfaction.[7]

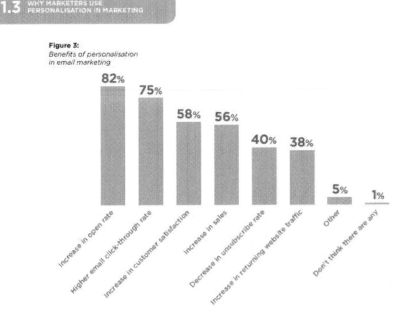

1.3 WHY MARKETERS USE
PERSONALISATION IN MARKETING

Figure 3:
*Benefits of personalisation
in email marketing*

*theidm.com/uploads/ckeditor/33805/IDM-Personalisation
-Research-Doc_v2.pdf*

When segmenting your list, it's important to think about div-vying it up by **interest**. The beauty of segmentation is you can build your prospect's interest over time—so someday they *might* graduate to interest in your offers, too.

Any good email tool these days has features to help you segment your list, often automatically. For example, you can set it up so when a user subscribes to your email newsletter from a page about SEO writing, they're automatically placed on a list of people interested in SEO writing, and a sequence triggered to nurture their potential of turning into a sale. This automation can be repeated for most other scenarios, wherever your user displays interest through an action they take on your site. It all depends on the email marketing tool you use and the available features of that tool.

👉 I discuss email segmentation and automation in greater depth in **Stage 2: Email Content Publishing.**

Just like any other type of content, email content should begin and end with your audience. Research them, talk to them, understand them, and you'll create great emails they'll be excited to open and read.

👉 My favorite email newsletters strike a perfect balance between how they target readers and the value they offer. Check out The Tilt *(thetilt.com)* and Daily Stoic (*dailystoic.com*) to see what I mean.

🔨 **Tools to use at this sub-stage:**

- Email marketing tool (There are a TON to choose from, and many are free or free to try—for a list of recs, check **Stage 2: Email Content Publishing >> Sub-Stage 2: Sending to Your List**)

Sub-Stage 2: Goals

Sending out great emails can and should help your brand grow. Verbalizing and recording the goals you want to advance will help you stay laser-focused.

 Delegate? NO—know your brand goals.

What do you want those emails to do for your brand? How do you want them to work for you? This is important to acknowledge right at the outset, before you send anything to anyone.

Establishing goals for your email content also gives you focus and purpose. For example, maybe you want your emails to help grow brand trust. In that case, sending out a weekly newsletter or digest might help you advance toward that. Or, perhaps you're looking for more sales or conversions from your emails. In that case, sending out targeted email sequences with an offer tied to them can help you get there. Or, maybe you want to drum up more interest and traffic to your blog content. Sending out promotional emails tied to each blog is a great way to do *that.*

While you define your email goals, don't forget to also define what "success" will look like along the way. How will you measure whether you've reached your goalposts? What metrics will you track? For example, maybe initially you just want people to read your emails, period. Your goal could be to increase engagement and opens, so you could set the goal to get 30% of your total subscriber list to open your emails. To reach that goal, you might experiment with subject line composition and wording, how you begin each email, and the content structure and quality inside them. When you reach that goal, you could move on to set a more ambitious one—maybe X number of subscribers will click a link inside your email. Once you hit *that* goal, you could keep climbing the ladder—X number of subscribers will buy after clicking your offer in an email, etc.

If your brand has never sent out emails before, this is a good way to ensure you know how to crawl before you try to run. And, whatever your goals may be, they should tie into your larger content marketing strategy. *Want deep knowledge of the content strategy and marketing process I use for all of my sustainable businesses? Check out contenthacker.com/transformation.*

🔨 **Tools to use at this sub-stage:**

- Your content marketing strategy

- Your overarching brand goals

Sub-Stage 3: Write

Writing emails, especially email sequences and offers, is an art and a science. Unless you're an experienced writer yourself with lots of successful emails to back that up, D.I.Y. at your own risk.

📝 **Delegate? YES**—enlist an expert email writer or a direct response copywriter, who will be trained to write copy that gets conversions.

Writing emails is not for the faint of heart. Bad or just plain *wrong* email content sent to your list can actually hurt your brand—it will send people running *from* you, not toward you.

Remember: Your brand presence is not made up of whatever bits and pieces you think are most important. Instead, it's an amalgamation, a composite of every little thing you do online and offline, every little thing you push out into the world, every word or string of text you publish. That includes your email content: your subject lines, your greetings, your messages, your CTAs, and even your closing signatures. (The difference between using "Sincerely," or "With kind regards," or, heaven forbid, "See ya on the flip side!" can have an impact on how people view your brand—and no, I'm not kidding.)

If you have zero experience writing emails on behalf of a business, *don't do it*. There's too much you could get wrong.

Instead, find an expert email writer. *If you need a good writer yesterday, check out expresswriters.com.*

👉 Need tips on hiring and delegating to writers? Head back to **Chapter 2**. Need guidance on creating a brief for a writer? Return to the first section in this chapter: ***Your Website and Blog*** >> ***Stage 1: Website & Blog Content Creation*** >> ***Sub-Stage 2: Ideate.***

🔨 Tools to use at this sub-stage:

- An expert writer!

Sub-Stage 4: Edit (A.K.A. Approval)

Every type of content needs a final check before it's sent into the world. This stage is where you potentially catch errors and mistakes that could hurt your image or alienate readers.

📝 **Delegate? MAYBE**—an editor could do the final once-over and ensure your emails are on-brand and consistent with your other content.

Since no one should know your audience and brand voice better than you, it's a good idea to run your expert eye over your emails before they go off into inboxes around the world. You'll instantly know whether some wording sounds off, if the message is too sales-y, or if the tone doesn't work *without* having to be an expert on email sequences or composition.

Plus, just like with your blog and website content, you may find opportunities to personalize your emails with a story, an anecdote, or some other tidbit your writer may not know. Keep in mind not *every* email needs this, but, if you see an opportunity, grab it.

Once you approve your email content, it's time to move on to Stage 2: Email Content Publishing.

🔨 **Tools to use at this sub-stage:**

- Your industry expert eye

- Your brand voice/tone guidelines

Stage 2: Email Content Publishing

Sub-Stage 1: Scheduling and Frequency

Learn how to send your emails—including both timing and frequency—so you don't turn off subscribers.

📝 **Delegate? MAYBE**—this is an easy and quick task to do yourself, if you want. If you'd rather free up your time, leave scheduling to your blog editor or social media manager.

How often should you send out emails? When should you send them? Short answer: It depends.

The long answer involves answering your questions with a question: What kinds of emails are you sending out? Use common sense regarding timing and frequency.

Email newsletters should go out on a set schedule, e.g. once a week, bi-weekly, once a month, etc.

Email sequences (also called "drip sequences") should go out on a one-time schedule, e.g. after the sequence is triggered, you send one email every two days until the sequence is finished, or one email every five days, etc. If you use an email automation tool, you won't need to worry about this—you can set up your sequence, then let it fly. Whenever someone completes an action triggering the sequence (you specify the action, whether a prospect signs up for your newsletter or leaves unpurchased items in their cart), it will run automatically. (More on this in the next sub-section.)

Blog promotion emails should go out right after the blog you want to promote has been published.

One-off email offers should coincide with deals, discounts, or coupons you offer. (Send more urgent emails the closer the deal gets to expiring.)

However, there's one caveat to all this you need to know. Do not, by any means, make the mistake of **email overkill**. Don't send your list so many messages that they get tired of you, fast. Don't give them brand fatigue. More emails do NOT equate to more interest. According to one study, 45.8% of subscribers flagged brand emails as spam because the brand emailed them too often.[8]

Instead, **let your list breathe**. For example, the maximum number of times most B2B marketers contact their subscribers is 2-3 times per month.[9] That's it! For B2C, that frequency increases to once per week *at most*.[10] To determine your own optimal email frequency, think about your industry, your niche, customer expectations, the value in each email you want to send, and your goals. You can even test different frequencies with different segments of subscribers to see how they respond and what works best.

Bottom line: There is no perfect frequency for sending emails. Every brand and every corresponding audience is different. Learn what works best for your particular situation and do your best to make each email valuable and worth opening. Never spam, and you'll be just fine.

Tools to use at this sub-stage:

- Email marketing tool (ConvertKit, Mailchimp, AWeber, GetResponse, Lead Pages—there are a TON to choose from, and many are free)

- Your intimate knowledge of your audience and industry

Sub-Stage 2: Sending to Your List

Email automation and sequences make your email strategy— and your life—MUCH easier.

Delegate? YES—determine scheduling and frequency first, then leave the physical act of sending out your messages to your email automation tool!

Just one of the many reasons to love email is how much control you have over the entire operation—including when and how you send out your emails. YOU are in charge of the experience your subscriber or prospect has with your emails, from the moment they read the subject line to the minute they engage with the content inside.

For finer control—for example, determining exactly when your emails will go out down to the second—you need to be using the tools and technology available right now. Think about sequences and automation, and use tools that help you implement them.

Email Sequences (or Drip Sequences)

As we discussed, email sequences are a series of emails sent out over a specified period. A sequence is triggered by a customer action, such as subscribing to your newsletter, and results in a series of emails sent out on a schedule. Each email helps pull your lead, prospect, subscriber—whatever you want to call them—closer to your brand.

Email sequences can have various goals attached. For instance, perhaps you just want to onboard new email subscribers to your list, introduce them to your brand and what you're about, and help them discover some relevant content they might enjoy. In short, you want to build up some trust and brand awareness. That's great!

Another common goal of an email sequence is to build up your customer's trust throughout the sequence so they pull the trigger on a specific offer. The offer could be anything: buying a seat for one of your courses, purchasing a product, downloading an ebook, etc.

One caveat: For sequences to work well, they need to be utterly audience and value-focused. That's because a sequence with an offer at the end can easily head into "slimy salesperson" territory, FAST, if you're not careful. It's really easy to lose sight of your prospect and lean into that "SELL, SELL, SELL" mentality. Luckily, if you hire a good writer who knows their way around a successful email sequence, you can avoid this pitfall entirely.

Just so you can see what I mean when I say "slimy salesperson," check out this bad email example:

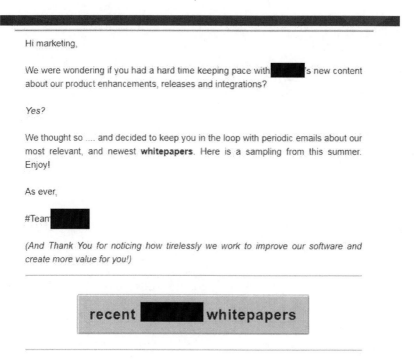

Hi marketing,

We were wondering if you had a hard time keeping pace with [REDACTED]'s new content about our product enhancements, releases and integrations?

Yes?

We thought so .... and decided to keep you in the loop with periodic emails about our most relevant, and newest **whitepapers**. Here is a sampling from this summer. Enjoy!

As ever,

#Team [REDACTED]

(And Thank You for noticing how tirelessly we work to improve our software and create more value for you!)

recent [REDACTED] whitepapers

More terrible emails here: nutshell.com/blog/worst-cold-emails-ever

Forget that this is addressed to "marketing," first of all. The most glaring problem here is the use of the word "we." *We, we, WE.* (You'd think we were reading "This Little Piggy Went to Market.") This email is all about the company, NOT about the subscriber/prospect. They even have the gumption to give themselves a pat on the back in the postscript ("Thanks for noticing OUR AWESOMENESS," is basically what they're saying. Ick.) This email is a perfect example of what NOT to do while crafting any email, let alone setting up an email sequence.

Email Automation

One of the biggest benefits of using email automation is time savings. You'll save so much time using a tool versus manually scheduling every single email or manually creating or compiling lists of subscribers. Best of all, almost every part of email marketing can be automated.

Automation also helps your email strategy become incredibly targeted and personalized. Instead of mass-sending your emails to one group of subscribers, automation lets you target specific people at specific stages of their customer journey. Great example: Someone exchanges their email for a free download on your site about SEO writing. That means they'll probably be interested in more content on SEO writing, so the sign-up triggers an automated response where they're added to a segment of your list that gets specific updates, tips, and information about all of your content and products related to SEO writing. Meanwhile... you don't lift a finger.

Needless to say, automation can be powerful. Here are a few other great places to implement it:

- *When someone abandons a shopping cart on your site* – a gentle email reminder, maybe with a discount attached, could nudge them to buy.

- *When someone signs up to your email list* – a welcome email is a good way to guide them into the fold and point them to additional content they might enjoy.

- *When someone sends a customer service complaint or inquiry* – while they wait for a personal reply from your team, an automated email response that lets them know their message was received and explains your process for addressing complaints and fixing issues may help smooth things over.

🔨 Email Tools Worth Considering

Finally, you can't implement email automation without a great tool. I've already mentioned a few good options, but I'll also include a handy list here for reference.

Paid Tools:

- **ConvertKit** – *convertkit.com* – My tool of choice. An especially awesome tool if you mainly earn money through blogging and content creation.

- **Mailchimp** – *mailchimp.com* – An advanced yet easy-to-use platform. (They also offer a free plan.)

- **Autopilot** – *autopilotapp.com* – Includes email and marketing automation in one platform. It's also free to use for up to 2,000 subscribers.

- **Drip** – *drip.com* – Best for ecommerce businesses.

- **ActiveCampaign** – *activecampaign.com* – Includes a really cool, visual automation builder for not just email, but all kinds of marketing.

Free Tools:

- **HubSpot's Email Marketing Tool** – *hubspot.com/products/ marketing/email* – An easy-to-use tool with lots of handy features and templates.

- **Sender** – *sender.net* – Great for creating professional, designed newsletters without any HTML knowledge.

- **Omnisend** – *omnisend.com* – Perfect for small to medium-sized ecommerce businesses.

YouTube

If we know anything about video content, it's that audiences *love* it. Full stop.

85% of internet users in the U.S. watch online videos.[11] Plus, 82% of all internet traffic comes from streaming videos and down-loads,[12] and 84% of consumers said they were convinced to make a purchase or subscribe to a brand's service because of a video they watched.[13] My favorite reason to create video? Because *nothing* replaces a lead or prospect being able to **hear** and **see** you. And they can't get that from written content. The trust factor is undeniable.

Video content can be a great source of leads and sales for your brand—that is, if you do video the smart way. What's the "smart way" when it comes to video content?

Spend time creating your content for YouTube, hands-down. Here's the cold, hard truth: the average lifespan of a video on Instagram is 48 hours. The average lifespan on Facebook is five hours. Twitter, twenty minutes. TikTok, a few minutes. But YouTube? Try **30+ days.**

A few minutes. Twenty minutes. Five hours. 30+ days. How long do *you* want your content investment and work to last? Do you want to create content that only lasts for a second or a few hours—or do you want to create content *that lasts?* You should choose the latter whenever possible. Think less burnout, less masses of quantity, and more quality in leads and lifespan, when it comes to YouTube.

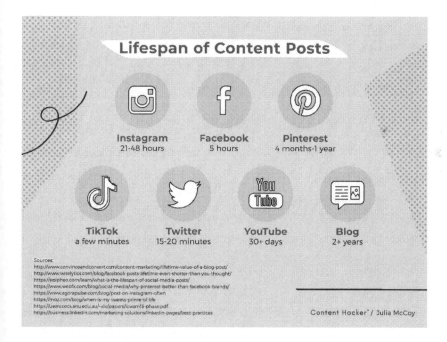

However, here's an important myth to bust when it comes to YouTube. Don't rely on YouTube exclusively for ad revenue.

Unless you have tens of thousands of subscribers, you *won't* make enough money to justify the time and investment. (I've been consistent at YouTube for five plus years, and the most I'm making in ad revenue is $90-$100 a month.)

Instead, think about YouTube as an additional vehicle for building brand awareness and finding new leads and clients. For most of us, our ideal leads are searching YouTube for content and answers, just like they're searching Google. That means, if you build a YouTube presence and invest in value-loaded videos there, you have a good shot at reaching them.

I'm a great example of this. I've worked on building my YouTube presence over time. Since 2017, I've invested in video production. By my third year, my channel got monetized and I started seeing real ROI from my efforts. What does "real ROI" look like? I bring in new clients to my brands, like one who bought a $1,000 course right after watching a few of my videos! Compare that to my $100/month ad revenue income. If I focused exclusively on ad revenue as my main goal, I'd be hugely, hugely disappointed and look at YouTube as a failed endeavor. BUT—I haven't, and it's not. Instead, I'm now reaching who I want to reach, proving my expertise, providing help and answers, and so much more, just now in video format as well as my tried-and-true written format. To date, I've brought in five figures in sales from leads who found me on YouTube.

The key is to not burn yourself out on production. I won't lie: It's a LOT of work, a lot of effort, and a lot of planning. But all of that is necessary if you want to make your YouTube content creation successful and bring in that good ol' ROI.

As always, I want to share what I know with you: how to set up a video content creation pipeline while totally bypassing burnout. Here's how it breaks down:

Stage 1: YouTube Content Creation & Filming (Production)

- Sub-Stage 1: Choose a Theme & Identity for Your Channel

- Sub-Stage 2: Ideate YouTube Content Topics

- Sub-Stage 3: Consider YouTube SEO

- Sub-Stage 4: Outline Your Script

- Sub-Stage 5: Fill in the Blanks & Write the Script

- Sub-Stage 6: Start Filming!

Stage 2: YouTube Content Publishing (Post-Production)

- Sub-Stage 1: Edit and Send Footage to Producer

- Sub-Stage 2: Pre-Publishing Tasks & Checklist

Let's dive into the deep end!

Stage 1: YouTube Content Creation & Filming (Production)

Sub-Stage 1: Choose a Theme & Identity for Your Channel

Your channel theme + identity form the basis of your entire YouTube presence. Before you do anything else, nail down this vital element.

📝 Delegate? NO

Much like your brand identity, your YouTube channel identity needs to broadcast to viewers, loud and clear, exactly what you're all about: what you stand for, what topics you'll cover, what they can expect to see from you now and in the future. Your channel identity is your overarching "why"—*why* are you making video content? Who are you serving? What is your ultimate goal? The equation of your theme + identity is your roadmap to all of these questions.

That means every video you put out should fall under your identity + theme umbrella. This is KEY to producing a cohesive, optimized channel that will resonate with your target audience, lure them in, and give them a reason to keep watching.

If you're thinking, "There are too many fun topics to cover... There's no way I can stick to one theme!" That's a trap. Without a theme and focus to hone your presence, you'll be too broad to appeal to anyone. Your channel will be sloppy, incoherent, and confusing. Nobody will understand why you do YouTube or what you stand for, let alone your expertise. So, please, hone your channel focus, choose an identity, and stay within those boundaries you set. Naturally, doing YouTube for your business gives you a ready-made theme + identity at the outset. Since you want it to tie into your brand, choose one that corresponds with the subjects and topics your business is already known for, or what you want to be known for.

My channel's theme and identity are linked to my expertise and my brand identity via Content Hacker: powerful content marketing that grows a business. And, by the way, once I themed my channel, I saw a lot more traction on YouTube.

youtube.com/JuliaMcCoy

Another important element to note: My channel identity is all about my audience and how I can help them. Even though it shows and presents me, in the end, it's not about me at all. It's about the value, the opportunities I can present to my viewer and subscriber. If you can word your identity this way, it will be much more compelling to your target viewer. It will also remind you of one of the ultimate golden rules of great content: **Your user/reader/viewer is king/queen.** Not you. Not the content. *Not* your brand. (If anything, your brand is the servant in this fairy tale. *Your content serves your audience. You serve your audience.* The End.)

One of the ultimate golden rules of great content: Your user/reader/viewer is king/queen. Not you. Not the content. Not your brand.

🔨 Tools to use at this sub-stage:

- Your industry expertise

- Your knowledge of your brand

- Your content strategy

Sub-Stage 2: Ideate YouTube Content Topics

What should your videos actually be about? Time to ideate those content topics your audience will love.

Delegate? NO—I recommend never outsourcing ideation, no matter what kind of content you're producing.

Once you have a clear channel theme and identity, you also have a roadmap in front of you, telling you which content topics you should cover in your videos. Particularly, it's important to ideate topics from a combination of **research** and **expertise**. For one, we've already tied your expertise to your channel theme, so anything you create will naturally spring from that well. For another, you should never try to ideate content topics off the top of your head or pull them out of thin air like a magician. If you're merely guessing at what topics your audience would love to hear about, that's a big NOPE. You can never know this for sure—there are educated guesses, of course, but guessing will never compare to knowing 100%, which is what research will give you.

The intersection of your expertise + research is exactly where you want to land when ideating topics. If you focus on one over the other, you'll be off the mark more likely than not. Why? Because alone, they're too broad. For example, if your expertise is selling running shoes, that takes you nowhere. What *about* running shoes? What facets of this topic will your audience care about?

Research tells you. Specifically, research what your **audience** is telling you.

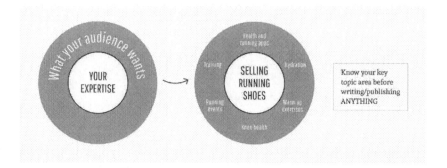

Look at conversations with your ideal prospects—what questions keep popping up in live chats on your website? What topics do you keep getting emails about? Is anyone asking questions in the comments on your social media posts? What about your DMs, your blog post comments, or Twitter chats? Research all of these areas, and, perhaps most importantly, LISTEN to what your audience says. They're your best source for content topics, hands-down.

🔨 **Tools to use at this sub-stage:**

• Knowledge of your audience and where they hang out online

• Audience data from brand interactions (email, chat, comments, etc.)

• Social listening

Sub-Stage 3: Consider YouTube SEO

Yes, you can and should optimize your YouTube videos with relevant keywords, descriptions, and titles for the best chance to appear in YouTube search AND suggested videos.

🗒 **Delegate? MAYBE**—a content strategist can do topic/keyword research for your video content if you'd rather not D.I.Y.

You've researched some audience-approved content topics that directly tie into your channel theme and identity, which in turn springs from your brand identity and expertise in your industry. Check, check, and check. It's not time to start scripting yet, however. First, for the best outcome, you must consider YouTube SEO.

Wait, what? How does that work? How do you optimize *videos* for SEO??

First, think about the fact that YouTube is the second most popular search engine in the world, right behind Google. Users around the globe stream one billion hours of video content every day.[14] YouTube gets more search volume than Yahoo!, Bing, Amazon, or Facebook.[15] And... people are searching YouTube with **keywords**.

That means you need to optimize your YouTube video content with keywords mapped to your content topic, placed in strategic spots on the video page (on top of relevant content inside the video itself):

- Video title

- Video description

- Tags

- Closed captions (CC)

Generally, aim for keywords that are relevant to your topic but have low competition (low search volume and a low keyword difficulty [KD] score).

👉 Return to **Chapter 4 >> Stage 1 >> Sub-Stage 1: Research** to get a refresher on keyword research! I cover this topic in-depth in my SEO writing course: seowritingcourse.com

Another factor that helps your videos rank, besides keywords? **Age**. As your videos age, they'll gain more views and traction, especially if you optimized properly at the outset, before publishing. A great example is a video of mine that now gets 1,000 new views weekly—but that traffic didn't start ratcheting up until a full *year* after it was published. Traction on YouTube takes time, but you already knew a good amount of patience goes into content marketing—and the returns compound over time!

🔨 Tools to use at this sub-stage:

- A YouTube SEO keyword research tool, or a keyword research tool with the ability to tap into YouTube search metrics. I highly recommend a tool like VidIQ – *vidiq.com*

Sub-Stage 4: Outline Your Script

As we've covered, outlining is an essential piece of the content creation process. This includes outlining your YouTube video scripts!

📝 **Delegate? NO**—especially if you'll be the one in front of the camera. Outlining—and the process of outlining!—helps order your thoughts and how you'll present them in your video.

Finally—time to dive into creating your video script! The first step, of course, is to create your outline. As we've discussed, outlines are very useful tools for content creation. They help you structure your content strategically so it's more engaging, understandable, clear, and concise. Outlining ensures you've included all the right information and used keywords correctly. Not to mention, an outline lets you play around with the inner workings of your content framework—the foundation, the support beams and footings, the walls and ceilings—*before* it's a bigger, unwieldy beast. You couldn't, for example, build a sound, solid house without blueprints. Similarly, you can't build a strong content piece, whether it's written, visual, or some other format, without a good underlying structure. The outline puts that structure in place.

A good outline leads to a great script, and a great script is a foundation for an incredible, ROI-worthy video.

Now, some of you might be tempted to skip the outline, and even the script, altogether. "Reading from a script will make me sound robotic," you might say. Or, "I'll sound more natural if I just improvise." But improvising would be a giant mistake, because outlining and scripting are what will keep you on-topic. They'll help you collect your thoughts and stay focused versus winging it and meandering down tangents your audience doesn't care about. Even if you don't read from your script word-for-word, even if you occasionally go off-script, you can still use it as a guide to help keep your talking points concise and to-the-point, and your video as a whole structured—so you don't end up with unusable footage of you rambling and "um"-ing for 10 minutes straight.

To this end, your outline can be as loose or as rigid as you want. You can simply outline the main talking points you'll cover, or you can go into more detail, summarize what you'll say about each point, add notes about effects or transitions you want to be aligned with your talking points, etc. Use whatever feels comfortable and ultimately helpful for you.

Also helpful: Divide your video into three chunks. The **intro** (your introduction, where you remind viewers of who you are and explain what's to come in your video), the **body content** (where you'll cover your topic in detail), and the **outro** (where you wrap up the video and sign off). Here's an example of how I outline my videos:

YouTube Video Script Template
Created by Julia McCoy of Express Writers
Subscribe to the Write Blog for more informative content around creating great content
(I know, #meta): https://expresswriters.com/write-blog

1. [Headline]

Example: What is Content Writing? How to Write 7 Timeless Types of Online Content

2. [Intro - remind them who you are + welcome them to the video topic]

Example Intro: Hey there! I'm Julia McCoy, founder of Express Writers, content hacker, and author. And you're watching one of my how-to videos on content writing.

In today's video, I'm answering a big question -- what is content writing?

I'm covering how to write the seven types of timeless online content that apply directly to the online growth of a business. (In my first book, published back in 2016 called So You Think You Can Write, The Definitive Guide to Successful Online Content, I cover these seven types.)

The 7 types of content are:

1. **Web content**
2. **Blogging**
3. **Social media**
4. **Ad and sales copy**
5. **Expert, or industry writing**
6. **journalistic/news writing**
7. **Creative writing**

Watch as I explain all seven types, how they apply specifically to an online business presence today, and how writers can grow their experience and income by learning these content formats.

This segment can double as a 59-second 'cut' to upload to social media (Instagram, Twitter, etc.)

3. [body content - 6-8 minutes]

See the video script for yourself (and download a copy to use!):
bit.ly/juliavideoscript

👉 Flip back to **Chapter 4 >> Stage 1 >> Substage 2: Ideation** for more guidance on outlining your content—especially if you plan on sending that outline over to a writer to flesh out.

🔨 **Tools to use at this sub-stage:**

- See tools from sub-stages #1-3

Sub-Stage 5: Fill in the Blanks & Write the Script

It's time to write that video script! Since you've already created an outline, this part should be fairly straightforward. You can also delegate to a writer at this point.

📝 **Delegate? MAYBE**—hand off your outline to a video script writer if you want to save time.

Scripting can seem pretty daunting at the outset, but it's not—I promise. Instead, at this point, scripting your video is as simple as pulling up your outline and filling in the blanks. Add details and flesh out what you'll say in each part. Expand on your key points. Write down the gist of what you want to say or script it out line by line—it's up to you. Write down stuff you absolutely don't want to forget to talk about. Your script is a tool that will help you make a better video, so take the time to plan it out.

At this point, you can also add more details specific to the video/ visual medium. For example, do you want a photo, screenshot, or URL to be displayed onscreen at a certain point? Add notes to your outline in these key places.

Conversely, If you're ready to hand off scripting to a writer, feel free to do that, too. If the writer you hired previously for blog and website content has experience writing video scripts, you can rely on them. However, keep in mind you might need to find a different expert if your go-to writer isn't a jack- (or jane-) of-all-trades. You don't want to hand off this type of task to a newbie UNLESS you're training them to handle it in the future.

⚒ Tools to use at this sub-stage:

- Your video outline from sub-stage #4

- Your expert video script writer (optional)

Sub-Stage 6: Start Filming!

Surprisingly, this sub-stage might be the hardest one. Don't worry—as you film more videos, you'll get better and better (not to mention faster) at hitting "record" and nailing it in a few takes.

📝 **Delegate? MAYBE**—but keep in mind lower budgets demand D.I.Y. video. Newbies should never delegate filming—huge waste of money.

Filming videos is *hard*. Especially if you're not used to being in front of a camera. But, just like anything else, practice makes perfect. The more you film, the easier it will get. But here's my BIG disclaimer, if you're new to this rigamarole:

It's going to be hard at first. It's going to take you a long time to feel natural whenever you push "record." You'll need lots of takes. You'll forget what you want to say, flub your script, and mess up. A LOT. Five years ago, when I first started filming, it took me *eight hours* of starting and stopping, starting and stopping, over and over on an endless loop, to get 10 minutes of usable footage.

Eight *hours* of work for 10 minutes of video. Ouch.

The best thing you can do in this scenario? Just do it. Just push "record." No matter how many times you have to do it. If you truly want to reap the rewards of video content marketing, you just have to press on and get it done.

While we're at it, we must talk about equipment. What camera should you use? What software do you need? What about filming accessories like lights and props? Let's discuss.

Recommended Filming Equipment & Tools

For Your Filming Setup:

For every new YouTuber, one of my top tips is to create a static YouTube filming area in your home/office. This area is always set up like you're about to film, so you never have to mess with décor, props, lighting, etc. Just head to your "YouTube corner," sit down, and push "record"! This also helps you when creative lightning strikes. If you feel inspired to film, you won't lose that spark if your filming area is ready to go for you. Here are the necessities for your filming setup:

Lights – No budget for lights? Set up your camera in front of a natural light source, i.e. a window. I filmed near a simple window for YEARS before I invested in some "fancy" lights (which are actually super inexpensive). Here's what I use for the cool neon light effect in my more recent videos:

1. Ustellar 4 Pack 25W RGB LED Flood Lights Color Changing Indoor Outdoor Floodlights–*amzn.to/3sqTtQN*

2. HAHOME Waterproof Fairy String Lights,33Ft 100 LEDs Indoor and Outdoor Starry Lights in pink, purple, and blue x3–*amzn.to/39gke2Q*

Décor – The décor you use in your filming setup will help your videos look unique, personal to you and your brand, and more dynamic. Add some interest to the frame and fill in the background with books, your brand logo, colorful art, or personal items with meaning to you. Since I'm a content creator, in the background of my videos you'll spy stacks of books (including ones I wrote!), inspirational quotes, a coffee mug with my name, a personalized YouTube letter, and a marquee letter "J" I found on Amazon.

💡 Get links to *every* product I use in my office in my complete **ergonomic home office & décor guide: contenthacker.com/ ergonomicguide**

🎥 For Filming/Recording Videos:

No matter your budget, you can create professional-looking videos. I filmed all my videos on an iPhone for years before I invested in better equipment. While the quality difference is noticeable, my iPhone did a serviceable job as I built up my channel. There's zero shame in relying on your phone to shoot video while you grow your brand and channel. It's okay to use a cheap mic and free software to edit your footage. Do what you can with what you have, focus on building, and eventually, you'll be able to justify investing in better equipment. Here are some recommendations.

Camera for newbie YouTubers: Your smartphone camera will work just fine! For crisper quality, turn on your 4K camera (most smartphones these days have this option).

Smartphone tripod: If you film with a smartphone, you absolutely will need a tripod to get the crispest video quality, shake-free. I recommend the UltraPro 72" Inch Heavy-Duty Aluminum Camera Tripod with Universal Smartphone Mount–*amzn.to/2X-7Hc8t*

Camera for more advanced YouTubers: I didn't upgrade my filming camera until my channel got monetized. Once that happened, I upgraded to a Fujifilm X-T4 Mirrorless Digital Camera XF16-80mm Lens Kit—and I highly recommend it!–*amzn.to/39iSvi4*

Lighting for filming: In addition to lighting that spices up your background and filming area, I recommend investing in a ring light to help boost brightness in your video footage, say, if you need to film on a gloomy, cloudy day, or even if you need to film at night. I use the Neewer Ring Light Kit–*amzn.to/2J5w7Lh*

Lavalier mic: For the best sound in your videos, you need a mic. This particular mic clips to your shirt, captures great sound, and is cheap, too: Shotory's Professional Lavalier Microphone for iP-hone, Camera, PC, Android, Lavalier Lapel Microphone with USB Charging, Omnidirectional Lapel Mic–*amzn.to/3IVBlw5*

Adapter for mic: If you film with an iPhone, you'll need a head-phone-to-lightning adapter for your mic so you can plug it into your smartphone. I like this $8 one: *amzn.to/3IYiaSy*

🎥 For Editing Videos:

I minimally edit my videos before I send them off to my producer (more on this in *Stage 2: YouTube Content Publishing*). For cut-ting out unusable footage from your video files, I recommend **Apple iMovie**—especially if you film with a nicer camera that outputs massive video files. iMovie handles them with aplomb: *apple.com/imovie*

If you film with a smartphone, **TechSmith Camtasia** is a great editing tool. They offer a free trial if you want to test it out: *techsmith.com/download/camtasia*

Stage 2: YouTube Content Publishing (Post-Production)

Sub-Stage 1: Edit and Send Footage to Producer

Your video is filmed. At this point in the process, it's a good idea to do a preliminary edit before sending your final video file to your producer.

Delegate? YES

I haven't had the time to build up the skill of producing vid-eos. Most likely, you haven't either—and that's perfectly okay, despite what the coaching world will tell you. Outsourcing the production of your video footage to an expert will save you a *massive* amount of time. Plus, the result will be worth every penny, as they'll have the means to design and produce extras that would take you years to learn like illustrations, animations, dynamic text, and more that will help differentiate your videos from the masses.

Once you've edited out the no-no's (footage you don't want to include), send your footage to a video producer! A good video producer has a few qualities that will matter hugely to your process:

- **Timeliness** – They won't needlessly delay your production timeline. They work efficiently and get your video file back to you when they say they will. If you request revisions, they also get those back to you promptly.

- **Good communication** – They communicate well about questions and problems. They get back to you quickly.

- **Fair rates** – Their rates are fair for the service they provide. (Expect to pay $200 *minimum* for good video production.)

But, before you head straight from filming to sending the footage over to the expert, **you'll need to do some trimming of your own.** I always cut out any footage I don't want my producer to use in a video editing program like Apple's iMovie. (See the previous section for links and recommendations.) Once that's done, I send the file over along with my notes for editing and production (effects, overlays, music, etc. all get added in production!).

⚒ Tools to use at this sub-stage:

- Your raw video files from filming

- Video editing software (iMovie, TechSmith's Camtasia, etc.)

- Your video outline/script with notes

Psst... this magical guide contains the name and contact info of my YouTube producer!

Stop pulling out your hair and start delegating. Get the Process Map today: contenthacker.com/processmap

Sub-Stage 2: Pre-Publishing Tasks & Checklist

At this point, your producer should have sent back your final, shiny video file. It's time to work on your pre-publishing check-list in the days leading up to publishing!

 Delegate? MAYBE

Video Production Timeline

Great content—including video content—cannot be rushed. As we've seen from the content creation processes, stages, and steps I've laid out for a variety of content types in this book, content needs TIME, PLANNING, and a PROCESS to be truly incredible. Similarly, you can't produce and publish videos on the fly if you expect to get any results. Instead—and, by the way, this is one of the best ways to avoid burnout—stick to a schedule with lots of padding for the multitudes of tiny steps you need to take along the way. For each video you publish, plan on adhering to a **two-week timeline**. This timeline includes planning, outlining, scripting, filming, editing, producing, pre-publishing tasks, and publishing. Here's a rough schedule of how that maps out:

1 day: I come up with video topic ideas one day ahead of filming at a minimum, and use VidIQ Pro to research low-competition keywords on YouTube.

1 day: I create an outline the day of filming, so it's fresh in my mind as I film. I film and edit on the same day as outline day.

1 day: I edit out the footage I don't want my producer to produce. It takes me about a day, in-between the other tasks I have going on. I create a detailed list of text and effects I want my producer to add for me.

4-5 days: My producer gets the video with the production notes and gets to work.

1 day: I review final files and ask for any revisions if needed.

3 days: I schedule my video out on YouTube typically three days ahead of time. I like to publish later in the week, but I often test this and try earlier weekdays, too. The time of day really depends on your subscribers, where they're based, and when they're watching—which can change dramatically month after month.

Pre-Publishing Tasks & Checklist

Once your video is scheduled, it's time to work on little tasks that will help your video get found in YouTube searches and recommended videos. Don't skip this step! Pre-publishing tasks and checks are *vital* to the success of your final live video. Here's the checklist I use to ensure each of my videos is optimized and ready to go live:

🎥 Is Your Video Publish-Ready?

Does it have...

- A keyword-optimized **title**?

- A custom **description**, optimized with your keyword? (A writer can create this for you!)

- A video **thumbnail**? To stand out, get a custom thumbnail designed by your graphic designer.

- A scheduled **publish date and time**? (After you pick the day, let YouTube suggest the time.)

- A defined **audience**? (made for kids or not)

- **Tags**? Use your main, focus keyword as the first tag. Use synonymous keywords for the rest. I recommend 10-15 tags per video.

- **Closed captions (CC)**? These are super important to include so your videos are accessible to everyone. You can hire someone to create CC for your videos—see next section.

Here's an example of a description from one of my videos. At the top, I include a unique 100-150 word description particular to the video. At the bottom, I include an "about me" footer that generally stays the same, the only thing I alter is which training, book, or course I feature inside.

Here's an example of a video thumbnail. My graphic designer creates all of my thumbnails from raw photos I send her. You can get great thumbnails like these on Fiverr.com, or from personal recommendations in my Content Hacker Process Map.

🔨 Production Resources

As we've walked through this process, you can definitely see why you simply can't handle YouTube video production all on your own... unless, of course, you *want* all of your time eaten up by fiddling endlessly with processes outside of your expertise. (That earns a big "nope" from me.) If you want to do video right, delegating will save you over and over again. Delegate, and you won't burn out before you ever see any gains from investing in a YouTube channel for your brand.

I rely on a list of video production partners and resources, and this delegation is one of the main reasons I've seen any traction on YouTube. Sure, your content must be high-quality, but you also need extra touches sprinkled in to stand out from the crowd. The experts you hire on the back-end WILL help set you apart on the front-end.

- **Video producer**: find a video producer that has specific experience with YouTube video production, so they can insert those important Subscribe, Like, and other channel-boosting animations at the right times

- **B-roll footage, creative filmography, etc.**: my husband films most of my B roll; but for the footage we can't get, I hire a team local to Austin, Media Pouch, who do fabulous work: *mediapouch.com*

- **Closed Captions (CC):** I use an AI tool that is cheap, simple, and easy! Just upload your file, and it spits out a mostly accurate SRT file for closed captions for extraordinarily cheaper rates than you'll pay a human. **Sonix.ai** is the AI-caption writing resource I use.

Chapter 4 Wrap-Up

- For every single piece of content you want to guide into the world, there's a process you can follow—a repeatable, step-by-step plan you can use over and over again to create, publish, and promote it.

- This process uses your brainpower and planning chops, plus the super talents of the team you assemble and delegate to.

- » Content creation doesn't work without delegation. You can't do it all alone and *not* burn out.

- The 3 major content creation stages* are:

  - » Creation

  - » Publishing

  - » Promotion

  - » *with some variances depending on the content type

  - » Creating content in planned stages, with a roadmap to follow for each type (blog & web content, email content, and video/YouTube content) simplifies what at first looks like a complex, nearly impossible endeavor. With the roadmap, what seemed impossible becomes possible!

  - » Ease into the process. Refer to Chapters 1 & 2 to get your mindset right and begin figuring out how you'll delegate. Do this BEFORE diving into content creation.

  - » All of the content creation processes are repeatable. For every piece of content you create, follow the stages. Rinse and repeat.

  - » *Breathe.* You've got this!

  - » Action is the biggest differentiator between the successful vs. unsuccessful.

"Inaction breeds doubt and fear. Action breeds confidence and courage. If you want to conquer fear, do not sit home and think about it. Go out and get busy." **– Dale Carnegie**

Content Hacker® / Julia McCoy

Chapter 4 References

1. Yiyi Li & Ying Xe. "Is a Picture Worth a Thousand Words? An Empirical Study of Image Content and Social Media Engagement." (2019, Nov. 18). *Journal of Marketing Research.* https://doi.org/10.1177%2F0022243719881113

2. Samuel Gibbs. "How did email grow from messages between academics to a global epidemic?" (2016, Mar. 7). *The Guardian.* https://www.theguardian.com/technology/2016/mar/07/email-ray-tomlinson-history

3. Julia McCoy. "What Drives Brand Trust Today and Going Forward?" (2020, Dec. 4). Content Hacker. https://contenthacker.com/what-drives-brand-trust/

4. Campaign Monitor. "Ultimate Email Marketing Benchmarks for 2021: By Industry and Day." (2021). https://www.campaignmonitor.com/resources/guides/email-marketing-benchmarks/

5. Brian Dean. "Social Network Usage & Growth Statistics: How Many People Use Social Media in 2021?" (2021, Sept. 1). Backlinko. https://backlinko.com/social-media-users

6. Andy Crestodina. "New Blogging Statistics: Blogging still works, especially for the 10% of bloggers who do things very differently..." (2020, Aug.–Sept). Orbit Media Studios. https://www.orbitmedia.com/blog/blogging-statistics/

7. Adestra & IDM. "The state of digital personalisation in 2016." (2016). https://www.theidm.com/uploads/ckeditor/33805/IDM-Personalisation-Research-Doc_v2.pdf

8. Daniel Burstein. "Email Marketing Research Chart: Why subscribers flag email as spam." (2015, Mar. 24). Marketing Sherpa. https://www.marketingsherpa.com/article/chart/why-subscribers-flag-email-as-spam

9. Direct Marketing Association. "DMA Insight: Marketer email tracking study." (2017). https://dma.org.uk/uploads/misc/589c5b9eaaca9-marketer-email-tracking-report-2017_589c5b9eaabde.pdf

10. Dann Albright. "How Often Are Marketers Sending Email?" (2018, Aug. 8). *Databox & Seventh Sense*. https://databox.com/email-marketing-sending-frequency

11. Statista. "Percentage of internet users who watch online video content on any device as of January 2018, by country." (2021, Jan. 26). https://www.statista.com/statistics/272835/share-of-internet-users-who-watch-online-videos/

12. Cisco. "Cisco Annual Internet Report (2018-2023) White Paper." (2020, Mar. 9). https://www.cisco.com/c/en/us/solutions/collateral/executive-perspectives/annual-internet-report/white-paper-c11-741490.html

13. Wyzowl. "Video Marketing Statistics 2021: The State of Video Marketing." (2021). https://www.wyzowl.com/video-marketing-statistics/

14. Cristos Goodrow. "You know what's cool? A billion hours." (2017, Feb. 27). YouTube Official Blog. https://blog.youtube/news-and-events/you-know-whats-cool-billion-hours/

15. Rand Fishkin. "2018 Search Market Share: Myths vs. Realities of Google, Bing, Amazon, Facebook, DuckDuckGo, & More." (2018, Oct. 16). SparkToro. https://sparktoro.com/blog/2018-search-market-share-myths-vs-realities-of-google-bing-amazon-facebook-duckduckgo-more/

Conclusion.
YOU CAN DO THIS (AND SUCCEED MORE THAN YOU IMAGINE)

Whew! You made it.

~~Content Burnout:~~ **Create Content** *How Entrepreneurs Can Position Their Voice & Brand in the World Without Overload, Frustration, or Burnout* was and will continue to be an inspiration to you in your journey forward. Keep it handy. Highlight the important parts. Use sticky notes. Dog-ear this book. All of that is A-OK—this is a *manual,* not some book that gets dusty on your shelf. I created it with that goal in mind.

Remember, **content is a living, breathing thing.** It's much like a baby that will combust if left unattended long. However, also like a human baby, you have the chance to see it grow, thrive, and become something you're proud of, as you nurture it, invest time into it, give it the right nourishment and treat it with consistent care and respect. The beginning is hard. The end is joy. Stay around for the rewards from consistently showing up and getting great at content. Lessen your burnout with the practices you've learned and imbibed in this book.

Moving forward, the success of your content is totally up to you. And it doesn't have to be an ordeal.

Choose your content investments wisely, and don't be swayed by FOMO or the flashy object syndrome. Shut out the noise of hearsay and trends, unless they make sense for you and your specific business. Example of a well-meaning bit of advice that could have you distracted like crazy: *Hey, Jane, let's try Reels today! I heard Bob say he got 10,000 views last night!* ...whoa, full stop. *But did Bob get LEADS?!* Remember, the vanity bubble that thousands of views create will pop as soon as the next shiny thing shows up on the horizon. **What's better? The strong current of content you create on your website that has staying**

power, that will give your audience a place to safely sink their anchors. That river grows in strength daily, from a weak trickle of water to a thriving current of possibility.

Remember the lifespan of content ...

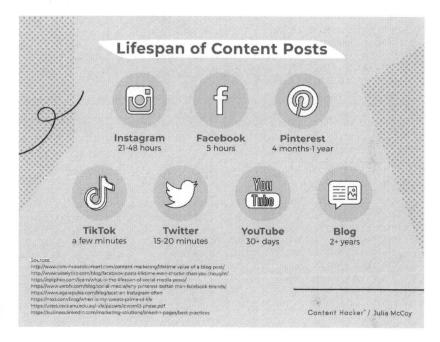

Written content on your internet real estate is your *best investment*.

Video content builds trust (prospects hear and see you) like *none other*.

A strategy keeps it fueled, *profitable*, MANAGEABLE... and a team keeps it going!

Let's review the steps one last time:

1. **Rethink content creation.** Throw everything you thought you knew out the window, and brace yourself for a major mindset shift. You can't implement content marketing by yourself if you expect it to earn its keep. You can't do it alone and not burn out. You need back-up! You also need concrete and clear **goals**, a strategic **plan** that outlines how you'll reach them, **partners** who will help you get your ship moving, and a desire to continually improve and **invest** back into your business. To rethink content creation, you'll need to:

   » ACCEPT your old methods don't work

   » DREAM of success in big, clear terms

   » WISE UP about how you'll reach that goal post

   » PARTNER UP with people who will help you get there

   » INVEST back into your business as you gain steam

2. **Start delegating.** Let go of total control in favor of building a solid team at your back who will help you produce incredible content every step of the way. Take care to find the right partners, train them thoroughly, and pay them well. You'll get back tenfold what you invest in your team. Finally, learn exactly what tasks in content creation to hand off and which ones you need to keep within your wheelhouse for ultimate efficiency, not to mention value, authenticity, and expertise in the content you offer your audience.

3. **Beat procrastination, and learn how to deal with it using mind/body techniques.** Burnout is closely linked to procrastination and depression. To truly beat burnout for good, you MUST understand the root causes and how to nip them in the bud. Getting your mindset right also means learning the habits, tools, and strategies that will lend the strength and resilience you need to overcome roadblocks like procrastination. Build good habits—both mental and physical—and you'll be able to build a way out of burnout if you ever find yourself there.

4. **Use repeatable content creation processes for each content type you want to publish.** You never, ever need to reinvent the wheel when the time comes to create content for your business (or for your clients' businesses). Instead, rely on proven processes you can repeat over and over, again and again, to produce amazing content that gets results. Generally, the overarching content creation roadmap involves three stages: **Creation**, **Publishing**, and **Promotion**. In turn, these can be broken down into sub-stages based on content type. Each person on your team fills a role at various stages. Tweak the sub-stages to fit your business and team as needed.

If you'd like my help and 1:1 coaching on all of these steps, consider sending in an application for my Content Transformation© Coaching System. It will change your life. contenthacker.com/transformation

If you're not sure you're ready for something this transformative, watch my free class on **How to Build YOUR Self-Sustaining**

Online Business in 90 Days WITHOUT Burnout from Overcomplicating It: contenthacker.com/freewebinar

If I could leave you with any last words, I would have to use two more aphorisms:

Slow and **steady wins** the race.
And a **car** gets you there much faster than your own two feet.

Slow, steady growth is *strong* growth. You're laying a foundation of brick instead of sand. You're putting out strong roots. You may have a sapling of a business now, but, with care, time, and attention, one day you'll be staring up at the towering redwood you grew from a tiny seedling. Content can absolutely help you get there, but only with the right mindset, strategies, delegation, and processes in place.

A car is the *vehicle* that gets you more quickly to growth. Instead of walking the same path for years, imagine being able to hop in the car and hit the highway much faster and zooming down the highway of legacy, profits, and freedom. That comes with the vehicle itself. Sometimes that looks like a coaching program. Sometimes that looks like a big investment in the process you need to build. (Find out what I think all the pieces of a self-sufficient business are in my free class, **How to Build YOUR Self-Sustaining Online Business in 90 Days WITHOUT Burnout from Overcomplicating It: contenthacker.com/freeclass**).

Lastly, remember: You can do *anything.* The choice is yours. And burnout should never be a default or a choice. *Freedom*, legacy, impact, should.

About the Author

Named a content marketing influencer and thought leader multiple times in the past decade, educator and author Julia McCoy is committed to helping people break out of the content ruts that stop success.

Seeking inspiration and a life led by her passions, Julia decided to follow her dream to write for a living at 19 years old. In 2011, three months after teaching herself online writing, Julia founded Express Writers.

She built her company to over $5M in gross revenue in the next decade completely through ad-free content marketing, serving clients like Johnson & Johnson and Nordstrom all the way to hundreds of small B2Bs. Her writing agency was one of the first in the industry to launch its own ecommerce platform for writers and clients. In 2020, Julia exited her agency in a private seven-figure sale.

Julia has been interviewed on Forbes multiple times, appeared on nearly 100 shows and publications, and spoken on the biggest stages in her industry, including Content Marketing World. Julia is the author of six bestselling books. Her memoir, Woman Rising: A True Story, pulls the curtain back on her unbelievable life story: how she escaped a Fundamentalist cult she was born in, and built a life of freedom, happiness and joy through her writing and content marketing career.

Post-agency exit, Julia is on a mission to serve a million entrepreneurs and give them the skills they need to successfully build, run, and grow their long-term online brand. At The Content Hacker™, through The Content Transformation System©, she's cultivating a new generation of content marketers — the mavericks, the radicals, the outside-the-box thinkers. Julia teaches, mentors, and leads her students, as well as takes the occasional pet project on herself: ghostwriting industry-changing books for visionary leaders. Subscribe to Julia's blog at contenthacker.com/blog, or if you're an audio person, sign up here for the Content Hacker podcast launching January 2022: contenthacker.com/podcast

Manufactured by Amazon.ca
Bolton, ON

25031252R00146